T0057358

THE FALL OF
A GREAT AMERICAN CITY

Kevin Baker

Foreword by James Howard Kunstler

City Point Press/*Harper's Magazine*

Co-published with *Harper's Magazine*, where an earlier version of this essay appeared in 2018.

City Point Press

P.O. Box 2063

Westport, CT 06880

www.citypointpress.com

Harper's Magazine Foundation

666 Broadway

New York, NY 10012

www.harpers.org

Distributed worldwide by Simon and Schuster

Hardcover ISBN 978-1-947951-14-3

eBook ISBN 978-1-947951-15-0

Cover and book design by Barbara Aronica-Buck

Photo research by Melissa Totten, M+Co

First Edition

Manufactured in Canada

For Anik and Jackson, native New Yorkers:
may the city shine for you again, as it did for me.

And as always,
For Ellen, with love.

Foreword

By James Howard Kunstler

Author of *The Geography of Nowhere*

The New York of my childhood was a deeply middle-class city. I grew up on the Upper East Side and went to the excellent Public School No. 6 on 82nd and Madison. Back in those days—the late 1950s—we little inmates of PS 6 were granted the freedom of the streets at noontime. The paranoia level around children was startlingly low back then. We knew how to get across a busy avenue at age 11, and how to order a hamburger with fries and a cherry coke at the Copper Lantern, and even how to get up to Yankee Stadium on a Saturday and buy a bleacher ticket without the help of a parent.

The school was one block from the Metropolitan Museum of Art, the Met. I often wandered up there during that lunch hour of glorious freedom. There was no shakedown at the entrance for "contributions." You just went in. On weekday afternoons, the place was pretty empty. Do you know why? Because most people were at work. This was before art became just another branch of show biz for the idle rich, and before the invention of the hedge fund.

My family lived in a seventeen-story pre-war apartment building on 68th Street and Second Avenue. Our place had two bedrooms, two baths (I had my own), and a working fireplace! We rented it for five hundred bucks a month. My stepfather was one of the "Mad Men" straight out of the cable TV show, a hard-drinking, witty public relations executive. My mother owned a shop on 72nd and Madison where she sold fancy stationery to the East Side lunch ladies. There were lots of people in Manhattan like my parents who lived in nice neighborhoods, went to Broadway plays, and had a little place on the beach somewhere during the summer.

Kevin Baker knows a lot about that lost city and what happened to it, and he tells the story of that metamorphosis really well in the wise and mordant howl of remonstration you are about to read. The difference between us is that I quit New York for good in 1966 and have lived mostly upstate ever since, and he stayed on to observe the mighty changes it endured—and to suffer the many discomforts of those changes.

I do visit the city regularly. One spring day recently, I walked across Central Park to the Met from my hotel near Lincoln Center. I was impressed to see what excellent condition the Park was in. The Sheep's Meadow was a lush greensward again, compared to the dusty hard-pan wasteland it had become in my youth. Many of Olmstead and Vaux's original buildings and furnishings, such as the Dairy, the Bethesda Fountain, and the Naumburg Bandshell, had been restored. This was a good thing, of course,

but it was also an obvious product of the extreme finan-
cialization of the economy that has insidiously concen-
trated much of the remaining wealth from asset-stripped
Flyover America into the dense canyons of New York City.

The Park, and the Central Park Conservancy that
now cares for it so meticulously, is a manifestation of all
that money flooding into Wall Street and its supporting
industries, as are the scores of new glass-curtain-wall condo
towers that serve as "investments" for plutocrats rather than
places to live. So is the gentrification of the many seedy old
neighborhoods like the Lower East Side, Soho, Tribeca,
the Meatpacking District, and, of course, the vast precincts
of Brooklyn—which were No-Go zones when I was in
high school, and as remote from my life as Czechoslovakia.

The life of a city pulsates through history as it moves
out of one cycle and into another. It brightens and dims and
repeats. I'd venture to say that the financialization-induced
super-high of recent decades has peaked. Many of the defor-
mations of city life that Kevin Baker mourns, such as the
empty shopfronts and the ghost condo towers, are symp-
toms of that. New York is stealthily entering uncharted
territory now, and I sense it will be much more of a struggle
going forward to maintain the expensive sheen it has
acquired and all the infrastructure needed to run it. I'm sure
there will be as much nostalgia for this incarnation of the
city as there is for my bygone, careworn New York of the
mid 20th century, in all its neurotic glory.

THE FALL OF
A GREAT AMERICAN CITY

Newsstand on Seventh Avenue near Penn Station, 2018.

Photograph © Jeremiah Moss/Jeremiah's Vanishing New York, 2018.

What happened to New York, the Great American City?

New York has been my home for more than forty years, from the year after the city's supposed nadir in 1975, when it nearly went bankrupt. I have lived through all the periods of boom and bust since, almost all of them related to the "paper economy" of finance and real estate speculation that took over the city long before it did the rest of the nation. But I have never seen what is going on now: the systematic, wholesale transformation of New York into a reserve of the obscenely wealthy and the barely here—a place increasingly devoid of the idiosyncrasy, the complexity, the opportunity, and the roiling excitement that make a city great.

As New York City enters the third decade of the twenty-first century, it is in imminent danger of becoming something it has never been before: unremarkable. It is approaching a state where it will no longer be a significant cultural entity but the world's largest gated community, with a few cupcake shops here and there.

For the first time in its history, New York is—well, *boring*.

This is not some new phenomenon but a cancer that's been metastasizing on the city for decades now. What's happening to New York now—what's already happened to most of Manhattan, its core—is happening in every American city of means. San Francisco is overrun by tech conjurers who are rapidly annihilating its remarkable diversity; they swarm in and out of the metropolis in specially chartered private buses to work in Silicon Valley, using the city itself as a gigantic bed-and-breakfast. People throw rocks at them, understandably. Boston, which used to be a city of a thousand ancient nooks and crannies, restaurants and shops, dive bars and ice cream parlors alike, all hidden down its alleyways and beneath its twisting, screeching elevated, is now one long, monotonous wall of modern skyscraper. In Washington, an army of cranes has transformed the city over the past twenty years, smoothing out all that was real and organic into a town of exclusive mausoleums for the Trump crowd to do its business in.

In trying to improve our cities, we have only succeeded in making them empty simulacra of what was. This should not be surprising, considering how we went about it. We signed on to political scams and mindless development schemes that are so grandiose that they have become even more destructive than the problems they were supposed to solve. This urban crisis of affluence only exemplifies our wider, continuing crisis: how we now live in an America where we believe that we no longer have any ability to control the systems we live under.

Those of us who have lived in New York for any amount of time are inevitably accused of yearning for the days of our youth if we dare to compare our shiny city of today unfavorably, in any way, to what came before.

So let me be perfectly clear, as that old New Yorker, Dick Nixon, used to say, and list here and now, in no particular order, all the things I hated about the New York of the '70s and '80s:

Crime.
Dirt.
Garbage left on the street for days.
Cockroaches.
The Bronx burning down.
Homelessness.

The discarded hypodermic needles on my building's stoop in the morning.

The discarded crack vials and packs of burned-out matches on my building's stoop in the morning.

The way cockroaches scatter everywhere when you turn on the light.

Entire neighborhoods of Brooklyn looking like bombed-out Dresden.

Subway cars covered in graffiti.

Subway cars on which only one door—or no door— opened when the train came in.

Subway cars ventilated in summer rush hours only by a single fan that swung slowly around and around, just stirring up the hot air.

Deindustrialization.

One World Trade Center.

Photograph © Andrew Nelson 2018.

The shabbiness of the old Times Square.

Those really big cockroaches that we called "water bugs" and that crunched like crack vials under your feet.

Okay?

What a city should be

Cities have always had more than one purpose. Places of protection, places of commerce: marketplaces, industrial nodes, citadels, the launching pads of trade that spans a continent and spans the world. Intellectual centers, melting pots, gorgeous mosaics, sanctuaries. Holy places.

Periodically, people have convinced themselves that we could do without cities—for example during the rush to the suburbs in the 1960s and '70s and, more recently, in dreaming up the web economy. They were wrong. Facing our growing environmental crisis, it is clear that we need cities more than ever to survive, and, no matter how connected we are electronically, we still need to connect face to face.

What makes a great modern city? It must be a place with a past—the past not only of its stones but of its peoples, a past they are aware of and that they honor, at least in some small ways. It must be a place of opportunity, but also of refuge. It should not be peaceful, but it must be a place of peace. It must consist at least in part of the particular and the peculiar, where one can see, all the time, things you don't see anywhere else, especially in our increasingly imposed, top-down society of today. Cities have long been one of the indispensable taproots of modern culture, where it is renewed and enhanced.

Cities are places of the mighty but also of the downtrodden, of those who opt out, and of the middle class. Cities must be places for workers, so that all who work among us can live among us, too, if they wish to.

For many years New York, like other great American cities, has been able to meet these standards, though not always perfectly, and not always all at once. Like those other cities, it has suffered its disasters and its bad years, been abused and scorned even by its own citizens, been robbed and neglected by its leaders. It has lost its way, and proceeded in pride or in ignorance, failing those who needed it the most. Terrible things can happen in cities.

Yet to move daily through the city is to see, everywhere, the fine threads that have held it together, and that should still bind us to it. Look around you, anywhere, and you can see something that cannot be reproduced today. Our system of public parks. The ornate façade of the American Museum of Natural History, with its world of wonders inside and its own shaded park outside. The stone-clad skyscrapers in their dignity and display. The palace for the people that is Grand Central Terminal. The institutions of learning that are everywhere, and the theatre district, unmatched anywhere in this hemisphere. The incredible underground networks that bring transport and heat and water to us all. The countless shops and cinemas and fine little restaurants, and apartment buildings that make up a neighborhood—and not just one neighborhood, but a thousand, repeated over and over again, each familiar but not the same, the mosaic that never repeats itself.

This is what ties a city together: bonds so elaborate and wound so tightly, over and over again, that it seems they can never be broken. And at the same time so delicate they can be cut before we even quite know it, leaving us grasping at what was.

The city—New York City, likely the most cosmopolitan city that ever was—is an amazing accomplishment, built by multitudes. But its luster is fading now. Its reason for being is fraying, along with those golden threads. Everything that seems most solid about the city, right down to its people, is in danger of coming apart, of dissolving into air.

New York today—*in the aggregate*—is probably a wealthier, healthier, cleaner, safer, less corrupt, and better run city than it has ever been. The same can be said for most of those other cities seen as recent urban success stories, from Los Angeles to Philadelphia, Portland to Atlanta.

But human beings don't live in the aggregate. And for all of its shiny new skin and its shiny new numbers, what's most amazing is how little of its social dysfunction New York has managed to shed over the past four decades.

Homelessness is at or near record levels. The Bronx, poster child for the bleakness of the city in the 1970s, remains the poorest urban county in the country, with almost 40 percent of the South Bronx, or more than a quarter-million people, still living below the poverty line. Prominent bus stop ads all over New York urge everyone to carry the emergency medication naloxone so they can reverse some of the opioid overdoses that killed *three New Yorkers a day* in 2016.

Most New Yorkers now work harder than ever, for less and less. Poverty in the city has lessened somewhat in the past few years, but through 2015 the official poverty rate was still at 19.9 percent, or nearly one in every five people. Those earning less than the "near-poverty" rate— families of four that earn $47,634 a year or less—make up *nearly half the city*, living what has become a subsistence existence, just one paycheck away from disaster. By comparison, the city's poverty rate in 1970—in the wake of Lyndon Johnson's War on Poverty—was just 11.5 percent. By 1975, during the alleged collapse of New York, it had increased to 15 percent, *still a figure lower than it has ever been since that time.*

In other words, all the decades of federal- and state-ordered austerity, all the "fiscal discipline" of our mayors and governors slicing away at "unaffordable" social programs and the wages of city workers, all the billions in tax "incentives" and other giveaways to attract and retain private enterprise, have resulted in a New York where economic survival for most of its people is more tenuous and harried than it was during the worst of our "bankruptcy" and "Sodom on the Hudson" days from forty years ago.

When you understand as well that, forty years ago, many households still did not have both adults working full-time, whether by choice or necessity, the difference becomes even starker. New Yorkers, aside from the aggregate, have been slowly slipping backward for decades.

The landlords are killing the town

The immediate cause of the "New Poverty" doesn't require much investigation. The landlords are killing the town. Long ago, the idea that rent is too damned high in New York became so thoroughly inculcated into the city's consciousness that it evolved into a one-man political party and a *Saturday Night Live* sketch. But the rent *is* too damned high, and getting higher all the time.

The average price to rent an apartment in New York reached $3,491 a month early in 2017, with those domiciles in new developments going for $4,963. Where the old rule-of-thumb was that your rent should not exceed one paycheck a month, or about 25 percent of your income, some 54.1 percent of New Yorkers now pay over 30 percent of their income in rent, and the trend is not good. From 2005 to 2015, while New Yorkers' incomes increased by just 1.9 percent, their rents—despite some of the most effective and

New York by Gehry.
Photograph © James Maher 2013.

far-reaching rent-stabilization statutes in the country—
went up by 13.8 percent. Even with the end of the Great
Recession, New York City rents rose twice as fast as wages
did from 2010 to 2017, and they rose fastest on the cheapest
apartments, rented by the lowest-wage earners in the city.

This is by no means only a New York phenomenon.
Rents are even higher in San Francisco and other cities in
the Bay Area, and Boston, San Diego, Honolulu, and
Miami are also rapidly pricing out anyone making what
used to be considered a living wage. Indeed, the cost of
affording a decent home is rapidly exceeding the grasp of
most Americans all over the country, not just in its most
desirable cities.

Cornell economist Robert Frank, by dint of his "Toil
Index," estimates that, where it took the median American
worker forty-five hours—or just a little more than that old
"one week's wage" standard—to earn a median urban,
monthly rent in 1950, as of 2011 it took *101 hours*, or over
two weeks. This is a social plague, one that is destroying
communities—and indeed, the very idea of community—
all over the United States.

"Wages and housing costs have diverged so dramati-
cally that, for a growing number of Americans, the dream
of a middle-class life has gone from difficult to impossible.
As I write this, there are only a dozen counties and one
metro area in America where a full-time minimum wage
worker can afford a one-bedroom apartment at fair market

rent," Jessica Bruder noted in her riveting (and often nightmarish) book *Nomadland: Surviving America in the Twenty-first Century,* in which she tracked the many Americans who have simply decided to give up on "sticks and bricks" and hit the road. "You'd have to make at least $16.35 an hour—more than twice the federal minimum wage— to rent such an apartment without spending more than the recommended 30 percent of income on housing. The consequences are dire, especially for the one in six American households that have been putting more than half of what they make into shelter. For many low-income families, that means little or nothing left over to buy food, medication, and other essentials."

As in so many things, though, New York is the same, only more so. New York City is the most expensive city in America, and if you subtract those people who live in public housing projects or other subsidized apartments, New Yorkers as of 2016 were spending on average almost 65.2 percent of their income on rent.

The entirely predictable result has been what New York journalist Michael Greenberg aptly called "the throes of a humanitarian emergency" in an August 2017 investigative piece for the *New York Review of Books.* Homelessness in the city has reached a level not seen here in decades, if ever. According to the latest figures, an average of 61,000 people are provided shelter every night, in 661 buildings, by the city's Department of Homeless Services. All told,

127,000 separate individuals slept in shelters in 2016—even though the city managed to find permanent housing for 38,000 homeless people in 2015.

Most of the "New Homeless" are not derelicts or the mentally ill. Three-quarters of these individuals are families with children, and at least one-third of the adults in these families hold jobs. They were simply priced out of a market that seems to have no ceiling.

Where most New Yorkers used to rent apartments of all sizes, more and more of the buildings their families made home for generations have been either torn down or replaced, or "converted" to condominiums or "cooperative apartments," which sound as though they should be something socialistic but are more like an eviction notice.

"If you need proof that Manhattan's real estate market has gone from 'pricey' to 'ridiculously out of reach' in the past decade," as Emily Nonko of ny.curbed wrote in 2018, then you need only consider how the average condo and co-op sale prices in Manhattan shot up past the $2 million mark for the first time ever the previous year, while a brownstone—usually a four-level house made from the lumpy brown stone that New Yorkers have for some reason come to adore—will cost you $6.28 million.

Good luck affording those.

SO WHAT ABOUT RENT CONTROL?

It is accepted wisdom, even in many liberal circles, that the cause of these outrageous rents and purchase prices is the very government intervention that was intended to ameliorate them: rent control. The argument, which sounds good on the surface, is that putting any kinds of controls on rents discourages developers who would otherwise, in their lemming-like greed, rush pell-mell into throwing up so many buildings they would drive the price of housing down.

Nothing could be further from the truth.

The notion that rent controls drive up rents might have some validity if, say, rent regulations in New York stifled construction. But they don't. *New* buildings in the city are subject to rent control only on those occasions when the developer agrees to it in return for some special subsidy. Builders have *always* been free in New York to erect a new building and charge whatever they want. More than 40,000 new buildings went up during Mayor Michael Bloomberg's twelve years in office (2002–2014), and another 25,000 were demolished.

The city continues today to furiously tear itself down and build itself back up again. New buildings are spiked into every available lot, and they rise higher than ever before. Far from discouraging new construction, New York's housing policies encourage and subsidize it at every turn—and, in doing so, they have only made the city less affordable than ever.

New York has had some sort of rent control continuously since 1943, and today nearly half of all its apartments—990,000 in all, containing 2.6 million of its 8.5–9 million people—are what is officially called "rent stabilized." That is, they are occupied by tenants in buildings of six or more units—rent stabilization doesn't apply to smaller buildings— who cannot be evicted or denied a lease renewal without due cause, and whose rents cannot be raised by more than a set amount that is decided upon every year by a government-appointed panel. Got it?

This does not mean that the rent doesn't go up. The rent on the rent-stabilized apartment that I've leased since 1980, for instance, has more than tripled and almost quadrupled in that time, which is not unusual. Rents can also be—*permanently*—raised when apartments are vacated, or when landlords make improvements to the building or to individual apartments. Or, if they are really determined to get more money out of their properties, landlords can wait until all their tenants' leases expire—they are almost never longer than one or two years—tear down their buildings and, once again, put up new buildings and new apartments for which they can charge whatever they want.

For that matter, once the monthly rent on a rent-stabilized apartment exceeds $2,700 a month, or if an apartment is vacated, or if the total household income exceeds $200,000 for two consecutive years, the unit usually passes out of rent stabilization. Forever. The result is that the number of stabilized apartments in the city has been steadily reduced. Just from 2008 to 2018, at least 172,000 New York apartments have been deregulated, a number that includes one-quarter of all apartments on the increasingly affluent Upper West Side of Manhattan, where I live.

The main culprits behind this deregulation are the private equity funds that see great possibilities in your neighborhood. In New York your landlord is now much less likely to be a family or an individual who has owned one or two buildings for years, depending on them for a safe and steady income, and much more likely to be a faceless, massively financed international firm that is highly incentivized to drive you out on the street and keep its investors happy. Whereas rent-stabilized buildings in New York once sold for about ten to twelve times what a landlord was likely to get back in a year's rent from the building, today they sell for thirty to forty times a year's rent— a purchase price a landlord will make back *only* if he fills the place with affluent renters or purchasers. This has led to predictable and often harrowing attempts

to speed up the process of emptying those apartments of tenants who might have the temerity to
think they are protected by the sanctity of a signed
contract, and the rule of law.

The mean-spirited city

On August 28, 2001, a small political miracle occurred,
unnoticed by most New Yorkers at the time and likely forgotten by those who did see it. In a televised debate a month
before the Democratic mayoral primary, four of the city's
leading elected officials squared off against each other—and
against a gaunt, 79-year-old perennial candidate and running enthusiast named George N. Spitz, inevitably
described in the papers as "a gadfly." But on this night, Spitz
spoke of the New York that had been, in terms of something
other than just fuzzy nostalgia or knee-jerk condemnation.

Evoking the city that he remembered from the Great
Depression—"a mean-spirited city compared to today [with]
one percent sales tax, no [city] income tax"—George Spitz
pointed out that that New York had nonetheless "built
Queens College, [built] Brooklyn College, libraries were
opened until nine every night, free tuition in the universities,
expanded park space fifty percent . . . ."

He noted in contrast that, in the New York of 2001,
even with "an eight-and-a-quarter-percent sales tax and a

huge income tax, we can't even pay our teachers properly, or police and fire properly. We pay them less than Bridgeport, Connecticut, or Newark, New Jersey [do]. The political culture is out of control."

Mr. Spitz was hastily told he was out of time, and resolutely ignored by the establishment (non-gadfly) candidates. But when WPIX, the local channel that broadcast the debate, took an immediate telephone poll after the debate, Spitz was the winner—with a mind-boggling 96 percent of the vote.

The result was quickly attributed to sunspots, or some similar atmospheric anomaly. Spitz's comments were ignored by the media, and his words were soon further buried by the events of 9/11 and its aftermath. Yet Spitz the gadfly had struck a nerve, raising questions that his long-tenured opponents had no ability to answer.

Spitz was invoking that old New York, from before the war and just after. The one which, even in its relative poverty, its corruption, and its "mean-spiritedness" was nevertheless a great middle-class city, offering a rich cultural life, opportunity, and diversion for all.

No more. The city's public amenities, built up for decades through the painstaking labors of so many dedicated individuals—working people and philanthropists, labor leaders and social workers, reformers and politicians—have now been torn away from the people. Look at almost any public service or space in the city, and you will see that it has been diminished, degraded, appropriated.

The change in their day-to-day life that had probably delighted New Yorkers the most over the past forty years was the vast improvement in the city's sprawling subway system. Ridership has approached record levels in recent years, and, on the first day of 2017, Gov. Andrew Cuomo led a giddy celebration to mark the opening of three new stations on the fabled "Second Avenue Subway," which finally became a (partial) reality after first being proposed in 1920.

The delirium and the self-congratulations proved short-lived, as service on the neglected system soon began to decline precipitously. An antiquated train signaling system—one that is not scheduled to be fully replaced until the year 2050, by which time the nanobots will have likely been doing the job for a generation—began causing longer and longer delays, with both cars and platforms filling up with frustrated, angry passengers. Some riders proved so desperate that they climbed out of the last car of trains stuck in the dark, rat-infested tunnels, braved the electrified third rails there, and made their way back to the previous stop on foot.

That June, an F train ended up stuck just outside a Brooklyn station when it lost power during rush hour. Commuters trapped in the steamy, darkened cars for over forty minutes stripped off clothing, attempted to pry the doors open with their hands, and wrote, "I WILL

SURVIVE!" with their fingers on the fogged-up window glass—a scene never witnessed even at the nadir of the struggling, graffitied subway system of the 1970s.

"The train was peeled open like a can opener," a transit worker said of a Harlem derailment that injured thirty-four riders just three weeks later, and left everyone else choking on a growing cloud of smoke as they tried to force the doors open.

The terrifying nature of the Harlem crash, in particular, finally got the authorities to pay some attention to how the subway had deteriorated. But less than a year later, in March 2018, passengers on rush hour G and F trains found themselves stranded between stations for two hours. Meanwhile, yet another fare hike was announced.

The problems of the subway are myriad and complex, not least of which is the fact that it is a 1904 system that remains open twenty-four hours a day. But as the *New York Times* found in an extensive investigative series stretching over months in 2017–2018, the main culprits were a perfect confluence of bad managerial decisions and ceaseless featherbedding: "Daily ridership has nearly doubled in the past two decades to nearly 5.7 million, but New York is the only major system in the world with fewer miles of track than it had during World War II. Efforts to add new lines have been hampered with generous agreements with labor unions and private contractors that have inflated construction costs to five times the international average."

In one of the many byzantine quirks of how we are governed in New York, the trains and buses are part of the Metropolitan Transportation Authority (MTA), which is controlled by Governor Cuomo, a Queens-born-and-bred third-term Democrat who has drawn almost his entire margin of victory from the city and downstate New York. But the ever-belligerent governor has proved strangely obdurate about addressing the subway's problems—even insisting that he is not really in charge of the MTA. For years, he resisted any efforts to find a dedicated funding source for the agency, even as the estimates of its unfunded capital needs rose to over $40 billion.

The grassroots, liberal election victories that swept the city in 2017 and 2018 forced Mr. Cuomo to at last pay attention, and to put his weight behind a "congestion pricing" plan to place a toll on drivers in perpetually gridlocked Lower Manhattan and dedicate that money to the MTA. But still, the overall reaction of the governor to the serious problems of the city's major modes of transportation seems weirdly arbitrary and unengaged, like politics out of an earlier, machine-dominated era.

When a demonstration appeared outside his Manhattan offices in the wake of the derailment, all Mr. Cuomo could think of to offer was a public contest, wherein anyone who came up with a great idea to make the trains run on time could win a million dollars. (The money, in the end, was awarded not to some future Thomas Edison but mostly in various grants to the city's existing transit contractors.)

The MTA had spent three years and countless work hours carefully preparing a plan to repair the foundation walls of the tunnel that carries the L train across the East River, from the Lower East Side of Manhattan to the Williamsburg section of Brooklyn—a tunnel which had been badly damaged by Hurricane Sandy in 2012. The authority had won the reluctant approval of local commuters for a plan that would have shut down the tunnel entirely—for reasons of both work speed and safety—for fifteen months, beginning in April 2019, and replacing the trains with a fleet of temporary express buses.

After a brief discussion with a disgruntled Williamsburg resident late in 2018, Gov. Cuomo scrapped these preparations. Following just three weeks of top-secret planning, he substituted a new plan that was announced at a January 3, 2019, press conference, with all of 11 minutes' prior notice to the MTA board, which he still insisted he did not control: "If they [the board] decide to pursue this alternative plan, great. If they decide not to pursue the alternative plan, make a decision, right?"

Unsurprisingly, the MTA chose Cuomo's plan, which was based on a new technique for tunnel repair that has been used in London and Hong Kong, but never in the United States, and which one board member had the mettle to suggest was more of a patchwork solution than the planned repairs, which were expected to last for fifty or sixty years. The Cuomo plan may well extend the time it takes to complete the repairs to at least twenty months, and is expected to still cause major, constant train delays, especially during the night hours.

It is, of course, fervently to be hoped that the Cuomo plan works in the tunnels that carry an estimated quarter-million people a day back and forth under the river. Yet there is something altogether frightening about how hastily and haphazardly it has been foisted upon us. It reminds one of nothing so much as the *old*, old mean-spirited city, of the 19th and early 20th centuries, when horrible calamities occurred regularly under the rule of Tammany Hall and other political machines, which in their rush to oblige wealth paid only the faintest attention to the public welfare. In one memorable instance, Tammany pols were even caught trying to sell faulty steel cables for the support of the Brooklyn Bridge.

No one, of course, suggests that Gov. Cuomo has some personal, Tammany-style stake in the L-line tunnel (and, even with the bad steel, the Brooklyn Bridge would have stayed up—probably). But the offhand nature of this way of dealing with the public is disconcerting—one more indication of a state and local government focused narrowly on the preservation of private wealth to the exclusion of all else, maybe even the public safety.

For the meantime, as the *Times* investigation concluded, "New York's subway now has the worst on-time performance of any major transit system in the world. . . . Just 65 percent of weekday trains reach their destinations on time, the lowest rate since . . . the transit crisis of the 1970s, when graffiti-covered cars regularly broke down."

"How are you going to represent beautify if you're doing ugly behind that?"

The decline of the subways is just the latest diminution of public life in New York. Over the last few decades, what used to be regarded as inviolate public space has been systematically rolled up and handed over to unelected private authorities. Starting with Central Park in 1980, much of New York's park system, once a jewel of urban innovation and social reform, has been handed over to privately funded "conservancies"—authorities supposedly subordinate to the city government, but in practice independent, all-powerful, and determined to put everything on a paying basis.

As an example of how this works politically, when the Republican national convention was held in New York in 2004, delegates were hosted at a gala in the Central Park Boathouse, while demonstrators were banned from the park—by the conservancy. On an everyday basis, what this means is that a visit to the Central Park Zoo, long completely free, now costs $12 per adult and $7 per child. A "Total Experience" ticket for the renowned Bronx Zoo costs $36.95 for all "adults" over the age of 12, $26.95 for younger children, and even $31.95 for seniors—in a borough where the median household income is $34,264. (Rental of a single-seat stroller will cost you $10. A wheelchair is free—but requires a $20 deposit, lest you attempt to speed off with it.)

Even the streets are no longer fully under public control. Beginning in 1982, New York created seventy-four "Business Improvement Districts" (BIDs), more than any other city in the country—although BIDs are now common in nearly every one of the nation's fifty largest metropolitan areas (and in ninety Wisconsin towns, under ex-Governor Scott Walker's accelerated privatization regimen). BIDs are supposed to be self-taxing coalitions of businesses, and in New York they have often been fêted for employing the homeless and destitute to pick up trash, prettify the streets, and man security patrols. But as the *New York Times* reported, one of the first New York BIDs instead "organized the workers into what were called 'goon squads' to use force to chase homeless people out of bank lobbies with A.T.M.s."

In 2000, the Grand Central Partnership and 34th Street Partnership BIDs finally settled a seven-year lawsuit charging that they had routinely paid their employees just $1 an hour to walk security patrols and clean toilets. The BIDs had dragged out the suit in the hope that their often homeless workers would simply give up and go away, but future Supreme Court Justice Sonia Sotomayor ruled that "the business districts had violated minimum wage laws, had used the cheap labor of so-called trainees to undercut competing companies, and had contributed the resulting profits to hefty executive salaries."

"You say you're doing so much for the city, but you're making that money off the backs of the homeless," Tommy Washington, then a 41-year-old former BID worker and plaintiff pointed out. "You donate lampposts, flower beds, Bryant Park. How are you going to represent beautify if you're doing ugly behind that?"

Mr. Washington's question goes to the heart of the new New York: whom it is for and what it means. Everywhere, private institutions have largely taken over the neighborhoods around them, repurposing them solely to meet their own needs.

The mirror city

Our tax-free universities have been among the worst offenders. Cooper Union abolished its legacy of free tuition after clotting the Astor Place area with ludicrously oversized glass boxes, and nearly driving itself into bankruptcy at the same time. This is not an insignificant institution or space in New York's history. Cooper was founded by Peter Cooper, a generous, self-made nineteenth-century industrialist and philanthropist who wanted to ensure that all working people had a chance at a good education. He created an after-work night school of the arts and sciences, one which quickly became not only an outstanding college but a cultural crossroads, famous for the speeches given by countless thinkers and leaders in its auditorium, including Lincoln's first address in the city and celebrated speeches by Frederick Douglass, Susan B. Anthony, Mark Twain and by Clara Lemlich, who called the women garment workers out to strike in the 1911 "Uprising of the Twenty Thousand."

Astor Place, for its part, was the site of the terrible and ludicrous (yes, events in New York can often be terrible *and* ludicrous) "Shakespeare Riots" of 1849, which may have left as many as thirty-one New Yorkers dead in the street and led people to profoundly rethink how hostile and alienated from each other our disparate economic classes had grown. Astor Place was deliberately redesigned to bring New Yorkers together, not only with Cooper Union, the workingman and workingwoman's college, but also subsidized housing, theatre for all, a lending library, and other public amenities. The public debate over how to distribute these benefits throughout the city even led to the creation of Central Park.

As in most of New York, the fortunes of Astor Place have ebbed and flowed over the years, but its basic legacy was still preserved, its essential space still extant. Then Cooper Union began to kill it. After keeping an area in the heart of the square as a dismal parking lot for decades,

51 Astor Place.
Photograph © Kenneth Grant/NewYorkitecture.com 2014.

the school sold it to Related Companies, the real estate giant, which proceeded to throw up Charles Gwathmey's monstrous "Sculpture for Living" at 445 Lafayette Street, a 21-story, sinuous glass-wall curtain that has been compared to a vertical suburban office park. The structure quickly became one of the most generally detested buildings in New York, but it would not hold that title for long, not even in Astor Place.

Exponentially more disturbing is Fumihiko Maki's 400,000-square-foot, $300-million, black glass box at 51 Astor Place, along the northeastern perimeter of the square, and now commonly known to New Yorkers as the "Death Star." The name is entirely apt. Maki's Death Star may well be the worst single act of vandalism in New York City since the original Pennsylvania Station was torn down in the 1960s. It is the final curtain, one that effectively obliterates what was once Astor Place.

I first came upon the Death Star after a long absence from the area. The change was startling. As it happened, there was some temporary artwork set up in the square, an entirely worthy sculpture of three rhinos balancing on each other to protest their near-extinction, but their presence— and their reflection in the looming black walls across the way—just added to the generally surreal feeling that everything here, everything of man and nature, was out of whack.

Cooper Union may be the worst academic despoiler of its own neighborhood, but it is far from the only one. New York University, in its own race against financial self-immolation, has torn down much of the historic West Village, including most of what was the landmark Provincetown Playhouse, and a home that Edgar Allen Poe once lived in, leaving only the door intact. (Quoth the raven: Fuck you.)

Columbia used (and abused) the power of eminent

domain to kick out residents and small businesses near the western end of 125th Street, and is now stuffing its new Manhattanville Campus there with still more glassy over-sized structures, courtesy of yet another rampaging star-chitect/vandal, Renzo Piano. The architectural critic James Gardner described his main building as "a hulking gray monolith . . . with almost nothing beautiful or delightful about it" that "evokes nothing," not even "any evocative tedium." This dreadful development—more like a blank, bland wall—will block what had been a lovely, almost pas-toral view of the Hudson River and the Palisades for riders on the elevated tracks of the No. 1 train in the interval where it rose briefly from the earth after West 116th Street.

But this also seems to be characteristic of the new city: the desire to curtain itself off. Luc Sante wrote in *Low Life* that "Manhattan was a theater from the first. When, early on, it was a walled city, and further surrounded by a forest of masts, it enclosed in its ring a small universe." As he also writes, "Manhattan has eternally been fascinated by itself," in its own, mast-rimmed theatre, but this was the splendid vanity of a proud city.

Today, in an oblivious city, it has been superseded by the vanity of the architects and their clients. We have wrapped ourselves so tightly around with figurative and literal mirrors—all that dark glass, reflecting us back at ourselves—that we cannot see anything else. Not far from where Columbia has cut us off from the river, on

Morningside Heights, the Episcopal Cathedral of St. John the Divine—the largest Gothic cathedral in the world—has chosen to wrap itself in luxury apartments for the sake of money. The cathedral began by sticking the merely awful 20-story Avalon Morningside Apartments tower in a corner of its sprawling grounds. But three years ago it went much further, allowing the truly appalling fifteen-story quasi-brutalist "Enclave" set of matching, glass and concrete towers so close to the cathedral's north walls that it might as well be situated in the choir loft.

I can well remember my first visit to St. John's, in September 1976. It was part of my very first class at Columbia, and our Art Humanities professor took us there to tell us how a cathedral worked, what it represented, and what it meant to the people who worshipped there. It was a thrilling experience for me, a joyous initiation to the larger world of knowledge and beauty that I was entering into in college, in New York—in a city.

One of the things I could understand immediately about cathedrals was why they were situated on hills when possible, to stand as a spiritual inspiration to material men. But now with St. John's, at least, it is impossible to see the cathedral in full at all, and will be for decades and maybe centuries. In its continuing quest for mammon, St. John's has also set up a literal glass paywall inside, so a visitor can no longer wander in awe past its chapels and under its magnificent vaulted ceilings, or stare into the eye of God represented by its great rose window—at least, not without paying $10 for adults, $8 for seniors and students (admission for lepers, the blind, and those possessed by spirits is unclear).

These are the crimes—the crimes against us all—that keep happening in New York now, almost without provoking comment. They can be perpetrated on something as grand as a cathedral and as small as a pleasing quotidian view. One of my favorite corners in Manhattan used to be West 43rd Street and Sixth Avenue, where one could see at the same time the Empire State Building and the Chrysler, two of the most gorgeous skyscrapers ever built. Then, more of the midtown glass towers now stuck willy-nilly into Midtown like pins plunged into a voodoo doll began to obscure the Chrysler Building. Soon it was gone.

The glassy new behemoths seem to have an unnatural hold on our power brokers. Mayor Michael Bloomberg did his best to replace or obscure much of "Terminal City"—the collection of older office buildings and hotels exquisitely designed to enhance Grand Central Terminal—with more gigantic, mindless glass super-towers, arguing that they would enable the communications economy of the future.

"With all those old buildings we have in aging Manhattan, we have to find a way to build modern buildings to compete with London, Singapore and Tokyo," gushed L. Jay Cross, president of Related Hudson Yards, on the opening of the first part of the overblown new complex he oversees.

Compete with them for what? The greatest number of giant, interchangeable buildings? And who exactly is "we" in this call to arms?

Enclave at the Cathedral.
Photograph courtesy of Handel Architects LLP/The Brodsky Organization.

We have blinded ourselves with mirrors. What is the point of building even the most beautiful buildings in the world, if no one can see them anymore? What is the point of preserving them? Or is *that* the point—that we will no longer want to preserve them, and the manic tearing down and building back up can resume without interruption?

This sporting life

Selling out has become an accepted way of proceeding in New York, not just for universities and tax-exempt churches, but for all sorts of subsidized institutions that are supposed to serve at least a semi-public purpose. Barclays Center at the Atlantic Yards in downtown Brooklyn was sold to the public in an elaborate bait-and-switch scheme, part of a spectacular "urban utopia" complex designed by Frank Gehry. It ended up instead as an arena with all the charm of your basic bus terminal, filled by an unwanted basketball team owned by a Russian oligarch. But then, in any major New York development today, some form of deception is almost requisite.

The Atlantic Yards scam was bankrolled with a total of $1.6 billion in public funding, including at least $100 million (and maybe considerably more) lost when the MTA—again!—sold its air rights to its train yards to the developer Forest City Ratner, which was the *low* bidder on the site. Before the whole charade was over, nearly 3,000 local low-rent residents were displaced from their homes; dozens of longtime neighborhood businesses were shuttered; and community, church, and labor leaders were corrupted with thinly veiled bribes. In a final, brilliant piece of political legerdemain, no elected official was forced to actually vote for the project.

Sports stadiums long ago became a preferred method of legalized graft in America, with even such struggling cities as Cleveland, Detroit, Oakland, and Baltimore shelling out hundreds of millions or even billions of dollars to retain or attract major league franchises. But once again, New York has exceeded all previous excesses. The new major league parks opened for the Yankees and the Mets in 2009 were far from the first or the only thumping public subsidies the city has given to those phenomenally wealthy franchises— a record of extortion and skullduggery that goes back decades. The city had already spent a combined $94 million building free minor league stadiums for both teams' farm clubs, in Staten Island and Coney Island, respectively. The current Yankee Stadium, erected on the site of what had been two beloved public parks dating back to 1897, cost $2.3 billion, making it (at the time) the second most expensive stadium ever built anywhere in the world.

Construction was helped along with federal, state, and local government subsidies totaling $1.2 billion. Nonetheless, the Yankees reduced the number of seats available to the general public by over 9,000, so that they could make room to raise the total number of luxury suites from sixteen to sixty. Even at that, the new stadium was so thoughtlessly and shabbily constructed that fans in the bleachers could not see the whole ballfield, thanks to a protruding luxury restaurant—Yankee Stadium's very own Death Star. Their views had to be assisted by video screens stuck on concrete walls.

It was much the same with the Mets' new park, out in Flushing's Willets Point, which hoovered up $616 million in total public subsidies but nonetheless reduced the new ballpark's seating capacity from 57,354 to a mere 41,800, while increasing its luxury suites from forty-five in the old Shea Stadium to fifty-four in the new Citi Field. But here, the new stadium was intended as only part of a grand plan by former Mayor Michael Bloomberg to transform the entire area around it. It was to be one anchor of an axis of redevelopment set to run across the entire width of the city, on a scale that only Robert Moses had previously attempted.

This is another rare quality of New York grandiosity. The overblown, depersonalized schemes of today are only following similar plans of yesteryear that were also supposed to put everything to rights.

Willets Point attained lasting literary fame in 1925 for its enormous dump, described by F. Scott Fitzgerald in *The Great Gatsby* as the forbidding "valley of ashes," where every day 100 boxcars piled the city's trash—mostly ash from its countless boiler rooms. Fantastical as it sounds, Fitzgerald was describing a real-life municipal dump, once ruled by the professional Tammany Hall character, John "Fishhooks" McCarthy, who was said to stop into Mass every morning and pray, "Lord, give us health and strength. We'll steal the rest."

Fishhooks and his dump were finally pushed out by Mayor Fiorello La Guardia and Robert Moses in 1935, as Moses tried to tie up *his* grand plan for New York first with a permanent world's fair, and then with the United Nations. When both of these schemes failed, Moses settled for Flushing Meadows Park and, eventually, the Mets' Shea Stadium. Just beyond the ballpark and the new tennis center in Flushing, in Willets Point itself, a happy jumble of some 250 small industrial shops, most of them specializing in auto parts and repairs, sprang up. They not only survived but prospered over the next eighty years in what became known as the "Iron Triangle," despite the city's refusal to build them sidewalks, paved roads, or even sewers.

Once the Mets had their new park, though, Mayor Michael Bloomberg looked to finally rid the city of these noisome, unsightly intruders where people actually worked. The Iron Triangle was to become "Willets West," a giant shopping mall with 200 stores and 1.7 million square feet of retail space, along with another 500,000 square feet of office space, a school, a movie theatre, 5,500 "market rate and affordable apartments," and even a marina for Flushing Bay.

To facilitate the process, $1 billion worth of public land was transferred, *gratis*, to two developers. One of these, Sterling Equities, is controlled by Mets owner Fred Wilpon and his brother-in-law, Saul Katz—the Wilpon family always being more interested in developing real estate than running a baseball club, as any Mets fan will tell you.

Something there is—maybe the shade of Fishhooks McCarthy—that resists the high life by Flushing Bay. A last-minute lawsuit succeeded in stopping this giveaway. Turns out that it's against the law to simply hand over public land without a specific act of the legislature—who knew?—and the fate of Willets West remains in limbo. But the Iron Triangle was already gone, its shops intimidated into closing by the threat of eminent domain, and then demolished by the city, another district of practical, working New York gone for good.

The Iron Triangle, now Citi Field, Willets Point, 2013.
Courtesy of Richard Levine / Alamy Stock Photo.

The axis of power

Queens had long remained unscathed by this sort of power development. More than anyplace else in New York, the borough retains some of the best of what New York was like in the 1970s, minus the crime and decay. Almost one in every two residents is foreign-born now, creating wonderful ethnic mixes in nearly all of its low-lying residential and industrial neighborhoods. But this cityscape is changing, too.

Much like the Martian spaceships from *The War of the Worlds*, in both appearance and annihilating intent, the glass skyscrapers that now dominate Manhattan have stepped across the East River. The first one, a 658-foot Citibank office building now known as One Court Square, arrived in Long Island City in 1989. For years it stood alone, an awkward sentinel among the neighborhood's eclectic mix of rowhouses, auto shops, and storied New York industrial enterprises—Silver Cup Bakery, Swingline staplers, Sunshine Biscuits, Mana cosmetics, Schick Technologies, and Eagle Electric with its famous electrified billboard promising, "PERFECTION IS NO ACCIDENT" (usually with several lightbulbs missing). There was even the world's largest fortune-cookie factory.

As these enterprises and more followed the siren call to parts of the globe where no one pays a living wage, a new wave of art, movie, and television studios filled their emptying factories and warehouses. Then in 1998 came the first residential towers, the forty-two-story Citylights residence, followed by the seven apartment buildings of the East Coast LIC complex. By 2015, the land rush—eagerly abetted by the city's massive rezoning—was on. In the year ending October 1, 2016, alone, seventeen office buildings, hotels, and residences between nine and fifty-eight stories high were added. At least four more towers of fifty to seventy-nine stories are planned or under construction, which between them will add 11,000 residences, 1,787 hotel rooms, and over a million feet in office space to the neighborhood. The tallest of them all is to be a $3 billion project with a luxury condo towering 700 feet high.

Yet even this runaway development is dwarfed by the western anchor of Bloomberg's great axis of power, Hudson Yards, the eastern part of which recently opened for business. The Yards is a project of staggering size, running from West 30th Street to West 42nd, and Twelfth Avenue to Eighth, encompassing some sixty blocks and twenty-eight acres along Manhattan's West Side—"the largest private development in the history of the United States and the largest development in New York City since Rockefeller Center," boasts its primary developer, once again Related Companies, though this time in collaboration with another of the world's largest developers, Oxford Properties.

Its angled glass skyscrapers are immense, overwhelming. From some angles, they look like battling "Transformers" from the movies, or blind, staggering glass men. From others, they seem, aptly enough, more like the smokestacks of an impossibly large steamship, about to shove off from the rest of the city altogether. Up close, they seem like merely a clutter of glass, channeling a heavy, perpetually whistling wind on the sightseers who fill its plazas.

"As Hudson Yards emerges, the neighborhood anticipates a collection of shops and restaurants that will welcome the world," boasts the Related Companies' brochure, confirming its intention to serve not really as a new part of New York City, but as another outpost of the world's glitterati.

The projected numbers, like those in Long Island City and even Willets Point, are numbing, almost too big to digest. By the time it's completed, Hudson Yards will encompass at least forty-three major buildings, with eighteen million square feet of commercial and residential space, one million square feet of retail and "mixed use space," a public school, at least one major hotel, and three parks. The ninety-two-story tower at 30 Hudson will boast the first open-air observation deck higher than that on the Empire State Building. Its tenants include a host of major corporations, while a seven-story shopping mall, The Shops and Restaurant at Hudson Yards (how imaginatively generic!), features a Neiman Marcus department store, the likes of Dior and Chanel on upper floors, and "a Fifth Avenue mix" of shops such as H&M, Zara, and Sephora on the lower floors—undoubtedly the first time that "Fifth Avenue" has been used to connote downscale retail spaces. (There will also be "seven destination restaurants" boasting "star chefs," for who is not a star in the wonderful new New York?)

"It is, at heart, a super-sized suburban-style office park, with a shopping mall and a quasi-gated community targeted at the 0.1 percent," appraised *New York Times* architectural critic Michael Kimmelman when the first half of the monster opened. "Hudson Yards glorifies a kind of surface spectacle, as if the peak ambitions of the city were consuming luxury goods and enjoying a smooth, seductive, mindless materialism."

Yet even more grotesque are the numbers on how much New York has spent or foregone in public monies to subsidize this monstrous growth. All in all, the development received $6 billion in public subsidies, according to the *Times'* 2019 investigation, or twice what Amazon was to receive in subsidies to build its controversial new headquarters in Queens.

That figure includes some $3.6 billion that is justifiable, supporting infrastructure: $1.2 billion to construct parks and open spaces, and another $2.4 billion to extend the No. 7 subway line from Times Square to the riverside, a long overdue improvement—although *not* one that should have been given priority over making the rest of the city's trains run on time.

But much of the rest is simply swag. Flaks for Hudson Yards throw around the usual fantastical figures for job creation—19,000! 55,000!—and claim it will all, ultimately, be "self-financing." That notion was exploded by scholars Bridget Fisher and Flávia Leite at the New School for Social Research, whose detailed study of the project found that the project will not be self-financing at all: $2.2 billion in taxpayer money will go to Hudson Yards' incredibly wealthy developers and their incredibly wealthy clients. None of it will create new net growth anytime soon—or maybe ever. Among other revelations, Fisher and Leite discovered that 90 *percent* of the office workers expected to fill Hudson Yards are likely to be employees from already flourishing corporate giants, moved a few blocks from their current offices in Midtown Manhattan.

"Black Rock, the world's largest money manager, which ended 2018 with $5.98 trillion under management, can obtain $25 million in state tax credits if it adds 700 jobs at Hudson Yards," reported Matthew Haag in the *Times*. Two major companies that will plant their headquarters in the complex will also get tax breaks: "L'Oréal USA is in line for $5.5 million for the same discretionary tax credit, while WarnerMedia can get $14 million."

Even companies that are not yet in Hudson Yards can benefit, according to Haag: "Future properties in Hudson Yards can also take advantage of the tax break, which can be as much as a 40 percent discount and last about 20 years."

Here is New York's 1970s mentality writ absurd. Stripped away is any pretense that we are jump-starting an important new development with a one-time subsidy. The city now promises to go on and on subsidizing its wealthiest companies and citizens, no matter how small the social benefit and how rich the beneficiary.

"We are still giving tax breaks to a development that enriches billionaire developers and high rise commercial and residential development that is not benefiting ordinary people in New York," laments James Parrott, a tireless advocate of sensible development who has fought the good fight for many years.

How did this happen? Like so many other developments in New York City today—the awful Nets' arena in Brooklyn, the dreadful over-development currently planned for Coney Island—it came about as a sort of bait-and-switch. For decades, New York's politicians and its ball-team owners suggested building a massive new stadium of some sort or another in this area, usually on a giant platform over the railyards to the west of the mutilated Penn Station. Ideas ranged from a suggestion for a new Polo Grounds for Willie Mays' old New York Giants, to Mayor Michael Bloomberg's proposal to bring the Olympics to the city.

The idea of a permanent West Side stadium appalled thinking New Yorkers, who understood that—the huge public cost aside—the traffic alone would bring Manhattan to a standstill on game or concert days. By comparison, a mixed-use housing-and-office complex—even a grotesquely oversized one—came to seem sensible.

Richard Ravitch, the legendary New York trouble-shooter who was the head of the MTA for a time in the 1980s, even boasted of purposely placing the tracks of the commuter marshaling yards far enough apart to accommodate pillars for some future platform. As it turned out, it was Stephen Ross of Related Companies who built it, at a cost of $1 billion.

Ravitch congratulated himself on the opening of Hudson Yards: "The M.T.A. didn't have the money, and it wasn't a priority [to build on the site]. Thank God it turned out to be a great success. It was worth what the city did for it."

But this is exactly the wrong way to approach development in any city. In the end, New York ended up subsidizing the rush of fantastically wealthy corporate giants toward *where they were wanted to go anyway*. For decades—after the wholesale transfer of the Port of New York to Newark and Elizabeth, New Jersey, began in the 1950s—the city has been moving toward its waterfronts. New York could have used the billions wasted on expediting this endeavor for improving local infrastructure, strengthening its educational system, making the streets safe—any number of useful projects.

In his withering review of a development that will define Manhattan's West Side for centuries to come, Michael Kimmelman asked rhetorically, "Is this the neighborhood New York deserves?"

Considering the lack of private vision or public involvement here, the answer, sadly, is yes.

Hudson Yards Futuristic Rendering, 2016.
Rendering courtesy of Related-Oxford.

The technology of the future

As gargantuan as these new developments are, for the powers that be they are not enough. Like Johnny Rocco, the gangster played by Edward G. Robinson in *Key Largo*, they never have got enough, and never will.

The city's politics were dominated in early 2019 not by any debate over its still struggling subway system, or its constantly rising rents and emptying storefronts, but by the quest to get Amazon to move to New York. The announcement that the distribution giant of the new gig economy would, indeed, place one of its two new East Coast "headquarters" in New York was made at an almost giddy press conference by Governor Cuomo and Mayor Bill de Blasio, able for once to put aside their petulant, childish squabbles, if only in such a bad cause.

Like all the best land grabs in New York, Amazon's subsidized move into a large chunk of Queens—complete with helipad for its founding deity, Jeff Bezos—was not subjected to anything like a vote by an elected, democratic institution, but okayed by the usual obscure and obliging state authorities. In return for its promise to bring at least 25,000—and maybe 40,000!—jobs paying an average of $150,000 apiece over the next twenty-five years, and to generate an estimated $27.5 billion in additional state and city revenue, Amazon was to receive an immediate $1.8 billion in state and city subsidies and tax breaks, and another

$1.2 billion when it produced the jobs. Greasing the way would be unspecified millions or billions more in further subsidies, such as federal tax breaks that would come from designating Long Island City a troubled "opportunity zone" under a new Trump tax plan.

It was, bubbled Andy Cuomo, "the highest rate of return for an economic incentive program the state has ever offered." During the extensive fourteen-month contest over Amazon—in which the company received mountains of economic data from New York and every other competing city, pure gold to the company under its business model and another *de facto* handout—Cuomo had even offered to change his name to "Amazon Cuomo" if the company came to his old home borough.

Mayor de Blasio, despite his election as the man who vowed to end New York's "tale of two cities" class divide, embraced the Amazon giveaway wholeheartedly as an "astounding return on investment" that would bring "literally an unprecedented number of jobs" and "blows away anything we've ever seen."

The most bald-faced aspect of the Amazon heist is how utterly transparent the lies are—apparently, even the lies told by the likes of de Blasio and Cuomo to themselves. The promises of job creation were generally the purest hooey, of the sort usually associated with subsidizing all those sports stadiums. We were informed, for instance, that the construction of Amazon's planned, four-million-square-foot campus on the East River would mean 1,300 construction jobs—this in a city where you cannot walk a block without tripping over a new skyscraper. Another risibly specific 107,000 "direct or indirect" jobs were also promised along with those 25,000 or 40,000 high-paying jobs that Amazon was to bestow upon us. These jobs could be anything or nothing—a part-time food server for a corporate luncheon, a security guard, a driver for a day— and who knows how many would have been created by whatever company moved into the space Amazon would occupy instead?

"Either you are part of the economy of the future, or you are part of the economy of yesterday," Cuomo decreed at his press conference, and there were other assurances from officials that "Amazon is the technology of the future."

But the dirty little secret about the "economy of the future" is that it's not about jobs.

Neither Andrew Cuomo nor Bill de Blasio nor Jeff Bezos nor God in His Heaven can honestly tell you that Amazon will or will not be employing 25,000 or 40,000 or any other number of highly paid workers in New York City in the year 2044. In fact, the entire focus of the "technology of the future" is on *removing* workers—both the workers in the countless smaller retail and online companies Amazon crushes on a daily basis, and within the company itself.

To get a good idea of just how this cruel and indifferent corporation operates, one can follow Jessica Bruder into a typical Amazon warehouse in *Nomadland*—a temporary job she took to accompany the homeless seniors she was writing about. Amazon avidly recruits these older workers because they are much less likely to complain about its brutal working conditions and low, low wages. Many of these seniors work 10-hour shifts in Amazon's cavernous, overheated or unheated warehouses, during which they "walk more than 15 miles on concrete floors, stooping, squatting, reaching, and climbing stairs as they scan, sort, and box merchandise," writes Bruder. If they *do* happen to complain about this mindless, numbing work—or if they have anything else to say, or if they simply miss a day or two due to exhaustion or illness—they are treated to "the Amazon Cold Shoulder" in which they are not formally fired or consulted in any way, but show up for work only to find that their electronic pass no longer opens the door to the warehouse. *Have a nice day!*

Amazon absolutely adores the sorts of aged, often desperate workers who will put up with this—but even so, the company is doing its level best to replace them. The warehouse workers must constantly accommodate Amazon's experimental robots, which at least provide amusement by failing so completely to do the modest tasks they are assigned. Often, they will end up simply handing items over to the snickering workers (probably not snickering too loudly). This is the other little secret about the "technology of the future": it doesn't work.

But of course, New York's leaders were not looking to bring anything so jejune as a warehouse and its workers to the city. These were to be the high earners, the people at the top driving the aged warehouse slaves, or the bin bots, or the drones that are the great, futuristic delivery ideas that Amazon has considered. This was to be another key feature of their Queens headquarters, the opportunity to live above and apart from the worker bees just as they work above and apart from them—and just as so many of the wealthiest New Yorkers already live as far above and apart from the rest of us as they can.

It is inherent in some of the concessions Amazon received, often presented as gifts to the city *from* the company. For instance, Deputy Mayor Alicia Glen announced that, over the next forty years, Amazon would make $600–$650 million in "PILOT" payments, or "Payments in Lieu of Taxes," to design its habitat's roads, sidewalks, parks, and other spaces—no doubt, just as it would like them. Amazon "agreed" to start a nifty, 600-student school in the neighborhood, complete with a "tech startup incubator"—undoubtedly intended to enroll the children of Amazon's executives, with likely some token number of local kids allowed to incubate as well. (The company *did* promise a whopping $5 million for "workforce development" programs, job fairs, and training at the nearby Queensbridge Houses public housing project—but with absolutely no guarantees of actual hires.)

This is, in general, exactly how *not* to "create" jobs for the New York of the future, another weird throwback to the desperate days of the 1970s and '80s, when filmmakers were shooting dystopic fantasies about the city, such as *The Warriors* and *Escape from New York*, and there was a scramble to attract business at any cost. Those days are long gone, but the city's Stockholm Syndrome mentality persists in its leaders.

Strangest of all is the fact that the site Amazon picked was in Long Island City, which is loading up with massive corporate and residential skyscrapers but still endures such inadequate infrastructure that local residents are advised not to flush their toilets when it rains. Never mind the sheer chicanery of declaring the community an "opportunity zone" so that money intended for truly depressed areas could be used to subsidize the richest single corporation in the world. (Amazon had planned to take the opportunity to initially move some of its operations into the space being vacated by Citigroup in its original One Court Square tower.)

The city did nothing of note, for decades, to keep the area's old manufacturing businesses—which employed thousands of working New Yorkers—from moving out. It also did nothing of note to aid the small businesses and artists that moved in to replace them. These would seem to be a much better bet on the future—and much better for actual, existing New Yorkers—than one giant company dedicated body and soul to *reducing* employment. It would also have helped existing New Yorkers, as opposed to begging a company to move in *with* many of its high-priced executives—thereby squeezing out many of those existing New Yorkers. (Again: New Yorkers would be hurt, but the city would benefit *in the aggregate.*) Even if Amazon's confabulated jobs creation numbers materialize—and it does not go up in a puff of smoke the way that so many other tech behemoths have—it would thereafter possess the power to extort any number of further concessions from the city's taxpayers by threatening to once again move on.

New York has had considerable success turning over big, abandoned old industrial facilities such as the Brooklyn Navy Yard to small businesses, and to artists and artisans of all kinds. It has also already attracted thousands of tech workers and executives through organizations as considerable as Google. Looking at these successes, it's easy to conclude that a much better strategy would be an "if you build it they will come" approach. Build up infrastructure, education, affordable housing, and transit, add them to an already exciting and diverse world city, and let companies compete over coming to New York, not the other way around. When they profit, let them pay real taxes, in lieu of nothing, that we will then all decide how to spend in the best interests of the whole city.

Instead, New York's political establishment insisted on acting as if they were running a Carolina mill town in the 1930s, flinging away subsidies that came to $48,000 per each (promised) job at Amazon. Opposition began to rise, led by local politicians and the Bronx and Queens' new congressional star, Rep. Alexandria Ocasio-Cortez, and by grassroots community organizations objecting to both the $3 billion thrown at Amazon and the whole undemocratic nature of the process.

"A deal created to fund one of the largest mega-projects in New York City's history without any public process, input, or deliberation not only disempowers the very communities that will be most impacted, but entirely erases their agency and their voices," pointed out the Association of Housing and Neighborhood Development.

Cuomo and de Blasio waved away all these objections to what was presented as a done deal. But Amazon's executives seemed stunned when they were sharply questioned at a City Council hearing. And when state senator Michael Gianaris, the most outspoken critic of the deal, was nominated to a spot on the Public Authorities Control Board—where he would have the power to singlehandedly veto the giveaway—rather than trying to make its case, Amazon abruptly gave New York the cold shoulder and announced that it would not be coming to the city after all. Its advocates had been sabotaged by their own democracy work-around.

Governor Cuomo and many of the other powers-that-be reacted like so many singed cats. Democratic State

Senate majority leader Andrea Stewart-Cousins quickly withdrew Gianaris's nomination to the Public Authorities Control Board. Cuomo made a personal appeal to Jeff Bezos while furiously denouncing the dissenters, and something calling itself the Partnership for New York City—described as a coalition that "represents the city's business leadership and its largest private sector employers"—ran a full-page ad in the *New York Times*, signed by dozens of business and union leaders and current and former politicos, shamelessly begging Amazon to reconsider. The *Times* itself ran a page-wide photograph mournfully depicting the parking lot and aged, empty infrastructure where Amazon was supposed to have its headquarters. (The picture was run letter-box style—only a couple of inches high, as if seen through a mailbox opening—which was apparently the only way the paper could crop out the forest of glistening new skyscrapers filling so much of the "opportunity zone.") The Mercer family, billionaire sponsors of the far right, even bought billboard space in Times Square denouncing Representative Ocasio-Cortez for her role in this tragedy. (It was located, without a hint of irony, just across 42nd Street from the Ripley's Believe It or Not! and Madame Tussauds waxworks emporia.)

Later, when a particularly scurrilous pollster asked New Yorkers all over the state to name the "chief villain" in Amazon's departure, the congresswoman came out the leader. (There was no word on who suggested the word "villain," but, if I had to guess, I'd say his initials would be A.C.)

Whether all this groveling will succeed in winning Jeff Bezos's forgiveness for the impertinence of some New Yorkers is as yet unknown. But the suspicion here is that, if this is forthcoming, it will have to be accompanied by even more in the way of handouts. If it is not, one can expect "Who lost Amazon?" to be waved in the face of every New Yorker who ever again dares to object to bribing fabulously wealthy people and companies to come to the city, much as "Who lost China?" became a rallying cry of the McCarthyists back in the 1950s.

Where I live

Things I liked about that old, vanished New York?

My neighbors.

Most of them are gone or going now, after decades in the same visibly slouching, ancient apartment house where I live. The apartment below mine, from the day I took possession in 1980 with three friends from college, was rented by Mercedes, an immigrant from the Dominican Republic, and her extended family of three generations. When her mother, Anna, a sunny, religious, and unfailingly kind woman, began to decline with the years, Mercedes tended to her devotedly at home, bringing a hospital bed into their living room. But their rent-controlled apartment was in Anna's name, and when she died, Mercedes and her husband could no longer afford even the stabilized rent, and decided to move back to the Dominican Republic. After all those years, they were just gone, almost overnight.

Across the hall from me was Raymond, a terribly self-destructive but amiable drunk, who fell completely apart when his mother died. He could not keep up the rent, or himself, and he was finally evicted and then banned from the block after several loud arguments with the super. He came back anyway, and lay down in the middle of the street one afternoon—a small Irish-Latino man in his perpetual baseball cap and scraggly beard, insisting in his gravelly, whiskey-soaked voice that they should just go ahead and run him over. Artie and James, our constant eyes on the street, who spend much of their time sitting out on the stoop trying to convince me that the Mets are a major-league ball team, waved off the traffic and persuaded him to get up out of the street. Forgiven by the super, Raymond now comes back to sit on the stoop with his old friends, a living ghost, haunting the block where he was born.

We are almost a joke about multiculturalism on our little street. Black and white, Hispanic and Asian; straight, gay and transsexual; families of every kind—extended, adopted, arranged by convenience and design. Protestant,

Empty storefronts on Broadway, May 2018.
Elizabeth Bick for Harper's Magazine.
Courtesy of the photographer. © 2018.

Catholic, Jewish, Hindu, Sikh, Buddhist. I used to come home and see the daughters of our Sikh mailman, before they grew up into gracious young women, playing baseball in the halls. In the evening, I sat at my desk in a little space, in this building cubbyholed with other little spaces, and held together by what was once described as "a hundred years of spit and dust," and felt as though I were poised over the center of the world. Beneath me I could hear a hive of dinnertime conversations carried on in half-a-dozen tongues, smell cooking dishes that came from all the ends of the earth, hear someone ringing a gong and repeating a Buddhist chant.

It is through these interactions, multiplied a million times over, that a truly great city is made. But now they are changing, fading. The street life—the warrens of little shops and businesses that once sustained our neighborhood in the "exuberant diversity" that Jane Jacobs considered a prerequisite to a successful city—is being eradicated as well, like the *botanica* on 96th Street that Susan, my sister-in-law, always visited to buy her healing herbs when she was in town and the Indian spice shop next to it with the protective elephant-headed idol of Ganesh mounted outside.

THE CITY INSIDE: LAST NIGHT AT SCALETTA'S

One of the most disorienting aspects of the New Affluence—in New York City, at least—is how hard it now is to find a first-rate restaurant in many neighborhoods. Or even an okay, good-for-a-Thursday-night-with-a-couple-old-friends place. Or even a dive bar.

"Scaletta's is part of their history—part of our family. Our grandkids', too. We've celebrated birthdays there, reunions, anniversaries," Bill Moyers reminisced in May of 2018, recalling how his grown children used to ask to go to Scaletta's on his—and my—Upper West Side.

No more. Moyers was informed that Scaletta Ristorante, a family favorite located for thirty years across West 77th Street from the American Museum of Natural History—itself about to be changed irretrievably—would soon be no more. While Scaletta's owners claimed it could make the astronomical new rent bill of $50,000 a month, it was ousted anyway for "a shinier, fancier model" desired by its landlord. A similar fate even befell one of New York's most revered power-lunch spots, The Four Seasons, Picasso curtain and all, when in 2016 it got the boot after more than half a century in its iconic location in the Seagram Building. Once again, the landlord wanted something hipper, something newer. Yeah, there's always another Picasso for the having.

Even when it's not about the money in New York, it's about the money. It's not enough anymore for an eatery—or a drinkery—to have a fabled and beloved past, or to serve fantastic food, or even to charge an arm and a leg. Now, restaurants must also be used to lure even more fabulous wealth—wealth that the landlords are sure is out there, no matter how many wonderful restaurants, shops, businesses, and family dreams they have to ruin to find it.

"The place was packed and people were lined up at the entrance waiting to get in. So many couples and families. The last homecoming. [Co-founder and co-owner] Freddie [Grgurev] came to say good-bye to us," Moyers related from his family's last night at Scaletta's. "He cried openly as he hugged my wife and me. 'You're part of the family,' he said. He must have repeated that scores of times across the evening, meaning it every time. Randy, the main waiter, brushed a tear from his eye. Our son asked him, 'What now, Randy?' He's a big guy, always steady on his feet. He looked away, shrugged, and said: 'I have to find a new job.' He's no spring chicken."

Moyers has enough perspective to realize this is far from a tragedy. Favorite restaurants, great restaurants—they come and go, much as they always have in New York. But he has noticed one family favorite after another —places such as Isabella's, a popular brunch spot, and Cherry's, nearby on Amsterdam Avenue—departing in recent years.

"We'll get something upscale and fancy, no doubt," he predicted. "But something like Scaletta's? Not at today's prices. There goes the neighborhood."

My wife and I have also mourned the loss of favorite restaurants over the years, such as Ouest, at Broadway and 84th, a place where we celebrated anniversaries, birthdays, family, and success for fourteen years, until it closed in 2015.

"We used to get the artists, writers, intellectuals, performers on a regular basis," the proprietor, Tom Valenti, was quoted as saying when Ouest went down. "But a lot of those Upper West Side old-timers, people like Sidney Lumet, are gone. And the new people in the big apartments have different interests."

Interests fancier than those of a big-time Hollywood director? Ouest was neither uncrowded nor cheap, and if it is to be considered *passé* just what do all "the new people in the big apartments" want? For that matter, the slew of standard Chinese restaurants that used to be in my immediate neighborhood—Hunan Balcony, Empire Szechuan—have closed as well, replaced by nothing or (much worse) a bank branch. All the dive bars I used to know and

love have gone down, too, with the death of the demi-
monde: the West End, up by Columbia, once famous
for its jazz, and where the Beats hung out in the
1940s, and the revolutionaries in the '60s. The Abbey
Pub, a few blocks away from where I live. The P&G
Café Bar on Amsterdam and West 73rd, closed in
2011 after sixty-six years and one scene in the movie
Donnie Brasco; the Emerald Inn at 69th and Columbus, where Jack Lemmon danced with Hope Holiday
on Christmas Eve in one unforgettable scene in *The
Apartment*. The Blue and Gold Tavern on the Lower
East Side and the Terminal Inn on the Upper East
Side; and the Grassroots and my beloved Holiday
Cocktail Lounge (see p. 129) on St. Marks Place; and
half a hundred more I have forgotten.

Not that dive bars are such a loss to the world,
either. But if there is no place even for expensive, elegant restaurants in New York, and no place for little
neighborhood restaurants, and no place for dive
bars—well, what exactly *is* there room for?

Or is this yet another example of the city being
shoved inside? Certainly, public dining in those restaurants that remain has become a more and more
aggravating experience in recent years, the music and
the general noise level cranked ever louder on the
well-known evolutionary evidence that, bombarded

by disturbing sounds, we mammals will eat and flee, thereby increasing diner turnover, increasing profits.

Is this one more example of the city's "practical pleasures," those small, useful joys like its cinemas and its bakeries and its shoe cobblers, all being suppressed because, economically, the space they occupy is deemed just too valuable? Is this one more notice being served that those who have the money can enjoy their Gaggenau kitchens and wine rooms, while the rest of us are deprived of yet another public space?

These stores, like so many others in my neighborhood, have not been replaced. They are simply . . . *gone*. In an informal survey of Broadway, from 93rd Street to 103rd, I recently counted 23 vacant storefronts—many of them very large spaces—enough to account for roughly one-third of the total street frontage. Nearly all of them have been empty now for months or even years.

Almost everything of use has gone. There was Oppenheimer's, a butcher shop whose eponymous founder had reportedly fled Nazi Germany and who brought his business down to our neighborhood from Washington Heights sometime in the 1940s. A large, imposing man with a bristling moustache, he would strut behind his counter like a Prussian field marshal, but he hired people of every color from the neighborhood, and left them to run the shop when he retired. Then, a few years ago,

West 85th Street, Upper West Side, Manhattan, 1986.
Photograph © Matt Weber 1986.

Oppenheimer's rent was tripled. Out it went. Over on Amsterdam, between 98th and 97th streets, were a whole row of enterprises: an excellent fish store, a Mexican restaurant named for Frida Kahlo, and a laundromat we used to call the "St. Launder Center," thanks to how part of its name had been torn out of its awning. Then they were all gone, too, without warning. Soon after, I ran into Shirley, doughty little Asian abbess of the St. Launder Center. She said the landlord had upped the rent from a hefty $7,000 a month to $21,000, which is a hell of a lot of laundry.

On the corner of 98th and Broadway is the shell of what was once RCI, an independent appliance store, founded in 1934 as "Radio Clinic." It was one of the oldest surviving businesses on the Upper West Side. RCI's proprietor, Leon Rubin, left the Russian Pale after his father was murdered there during the revolution, when Leon was just twelve years old. In his shop, he used to sit in the front window in a white doctor's smock, pretending to "operate" on malfunctioning radios. RCI was passed down to Leon's son, Alan, and changed with the times, stocking up on appliances, and electronics of all sorts. Alan's daughter, Jen, would demonstrate primitive Atari games in the same window where her grandfather had fiddled with radios.

"This was his family's business, and my dad wasn't budging," wrote Jen Rubin in her 2018 memoir of a family and a business, *We Are Staying*. RCI even survived being looted and vandalized during the blackout rioting in the summer of 1977—but it couldn't withstand today's Manhattan rents. The little shop lost its lease in 2014, the business chased off to Queens after eighty years in the neighborhood. Today, five years later, its storefront remains empty. Like so many other abandoned spaces along Broadway, its doorway has become a refuge for the homeless and the insane, supposedly purged from our city streets.

A couple of blocks north and across Broadway from RCI was the old Metro Theater, originally the Midtown, an aging art house that dated back to 1933, and that hung on long enough to become the second-oldest surviving cinema in New York. It had fallen on hard times, and was showing pornos when I first moved into the neighborhood—not a good fate, and one that symbolized too much of what New York had fallen to (and no, for the record, I don't miss the old Times Square, either). Then it was bought and restored by a repertory cinema impresario, Dan Talbot, who renamed it the Metro, burnished and restored its elegant Art Deco décor, and started showing old pictures and then contemporary second-run releases.

The restored Metro shined so brightly that it gained a cameo role in the 1986 film *Hannah and Her Sisters*, one of Woody Allen's most intricate and beautifully realized movies about the city. In the film, Allen's character, Mickey, weary of life and of love and having just botched a suicide attempt, walks out into a "violent and unreal" city.

"I wandered on the Upper West Side. It must have

been hours. My feet hurt, my head was pounding. I went into a movie. Didn't know what was playing," he relates in a voiceover.

The theatre he wanders into is the Metro, and on the screen he sees the Marx brothers and a vast supporting cast splendidly singing and shimmying through the "Captain Spaulding" number from *Animal Crackers*. It provides a revelation for Mickey:

"Look at all these people on the screen. They're laughing, and dancing, and having fun, and what if the worst is true? What if there is no God, and you only go around once, that's it? Don't you want to be part of the experience? It's not all a drag. And I'm thinking, 'I should stop ruining my life searching for answers and just enjoy it while it lasts.'"

This, too, is so much a part of what life was in New York: stopping into a movie theatre, any time of the day or night, and getting . . . a laugh. A nap. A reason to live, perhaps. The incidental city, in all its glory. And if this is almost a caricature of modern secular humanism—if it is almost a parody of self-referential urbanism, a native-born Jewish New York comedian finding, in the work of a family of Jewish New York comedians born not so far away from the very movie theatre where he's sitting, a reason to live—well, that's part of us, too.

Or at least, it used to be. Dan Talbot died in late 2017, just a month before another of his marvelous reclamations, the underground Lincoln Plaza Cinemas, another eccentric

Upper West Side institution and still extremely popular, was shuttered in some other, obscure real-estate shuffle. Gone was a movie house that had shown top foreign films and "art movies" to New Yorkers for a generation. There is barely anyplace left to see such rarities—once a common-place—anywhere in New York. A leading cultural venue in our greatest, most cosmopolitan city gone forever? Well, that's just the way it is.

The Metro had closed in 2005. Already struggling, it was all but enveloped by a massive construction project, Ariel East and Ariel West, two more glass-box, multi-million-dollar condo giants built directly across Broadway from each other. Rising to thirty-seven and thirty-one stories, respectively, they are related in size and style to nothing else at all in the neighborhood, looking instead like some fraudulent CGI enhancement in a bad science fiction movie. Their existence was enabled by the fact that St. Michael's, a charming Episcopal church on the corner of 99th Street and Amsterdam Avenue, sold its air rights to developers, much as St. John the Divine did just thirteen blocks uptown. In today's New York, for any older, under-capitalized institution, survival often involves cannibalizing the neighborhood it has pledged to serve.

The Metro never reopened. Its Art Deco marquee, and its purple-and-white terra-cotta tile work depicting the figures of comedy and tragedy, had been landmarked, but there was no such protection for the interior. The developers ripped it all out, gutted it too quickly for anyone to raise an objection. It has remained empty and moldering for fourteen years now, the letters of its name and other parts of the façade left to slowly drop off, piece by piece— perhaps on purpose, until there will be nothing left to land- mark. Online, neighborhood news sites pass on constant rumors about what the Metro is likely to become, but noth- ing has materialized.

"I was really hoping for another bank or chain drug store, or a combination bank/chain drug store," read one sarcastic reply to the latest conjecture.

In a city that boasts of being the capital of American theatre, and where dozens of striving theatre groups can't find a stage on which to perform, it might be thought that an empty cinema no one will rent would be a perfect venue for an Off-Off-Broadway playhouse. But that's not the sort of community improvement that most of New York's leaders even think of trying to influence into reality today.

These are the dwindling treasures of our existence in the city. Nothing so grand, just the framework of a life. If a movie theatre you can duck into in the middle of the day is one of the small raptures of the modern urban landscape, all around us were the same sorts of existential conven- iences. Those corner bakeries with the string-wrapped boxes where you could get a respectable layer cake on the way to someone's dinner party. A kosher butcher, where

Cup & Saucer Luncheonette, 2016.
Photograph © Paul Jarvie 2016.

you could pick up the lamb shank you realized you forgot just minutes before the family was due over for Passover dinner. Decent Chinese food for a Friday night sacked out at home in front of the television.

We worry now, in my neighborhood, that the cobbler's shop across Broadway will soon be priced out of business. In his shop windows, the proprietor proudly displays calendar photos of erupting volcanoes from his native Ecuador, alongside pictures of his grandkids at their confirmations. His grandson used to store his toys and his coloring books in the boxes under the unused shoeshine chairs. When you walk in, there is always the sound of classical music on the radio, and the smell of something very elemental and raw, leather and polish, the scent of a real place, serving a real purpose.

It is, almost, the only store around that provides anything of use anymore. There are a couple small hardware shops left still, some dry cleaners, a grocery store and a bodega, and a copy shop. But otherwise, Jane Jacobs's "intricate ballet of the streets" is being rapidly eradicated by a predatory monoculture. Everywhere, that which is universal and uniform prevails. On those same ten blocks of my neighborhood, I count now three pharmacies, six bank branches, seven nail-and-beauty salons, five phone-and-cable TV stores, four eyewear shops. Chain stores, of a type once unknown in New York, abound: two Dunkin' Donuts, three 7-Elevens, three Starbucks. The coming growth industry seems to be in urgent-care facilities, of which there are already two, to serve our ridiculously underinsured population.

Back to the urban chic

Where I live is not an anomaly. The problem is so pervasive, there are now so many empty shops that the issue has even begun to slip out from under the official, sternly reiterated doctrine that *New York has never been better than it is now.* In true *samizdat* style, an informal but growing network of dissident government officials, journalists, angry and frustrated private citizens, and even real estate developers started to force their dissent into the last, generally somnolent municipal elections in 2017. That June, the office of Manhattan Borough President Gale Brewer tallied 188 vacant storefronts along Broadway from Battery Park to Inwood. That number was almost certainly an undercount, but in any case it was tabulated on a main commercial avenue, in an incredibly wealthy city, in the eighth year of an economic expansion.

In 2017, Justin Levinson, a freelance software developer and longtime New Yorker, also began mapping commercial vacancies around Manhattan on his website, *Vacant New York.* He produced a black silhouette of Manhattan, studded with red blotches that each represented a vacant storefront. It might have been the cockpit view of some tormented city during a World War II bombing run (another ironic turn for a New York that was so often compared to "bombed-out Dresden" during "the bad old days"). Levinson found over a thousand vacancies—but also discovered in person "more than 100 [vacant] properties" missing from electronic databanks in the East Village and the Lower East Side alone, "meaning the rest of the city is almost certainly worse than it looks on the map.

"SoHo is a prime example; one of the most expensive shopping districts in the city is littered with vacancies. When I first built the map, I assumed this was some sort of [computer] bug," Levinson wrote, but after investigating in person, he found "it's as bad as the map looks. Circling one empty block yielded nine empty storefronts, most of them previously housing mid- to high-end national brands, including Helmut Lang (home of the $360 hoodie). If these stores can't survive, who can?"

Who indeed?

Jeremiah Moss's impassioned, uncompromising, often brilliant book, *Vanishing New York*, an extension of his blog by the same name, systematically traces the absurdities of how one neighborhood after another, throughout Manhattan, Brooklyn, Queens, and the Bronx, has been transformed by shopkeepers promising grungy urban chic that quickly proved to be little more than a parody of the city that they claimed to celebrate. (As previously mentioned, those of us who actually lived through the grungy urban chic didn't love it, we put up with it because of everything else the city offered—all of which is now being disappeared.)

Saddest of all the many very sad examples Moss relates is the planned demolition of the Essex Street

Market. It was one of a row of seven indoor markets built by Mayor La Guardia along Essex Street in 1940, back when the city endeavored to serve its people, instead of just weeding them out if they didn't make enough money. The Essex Street markets had been built to house the myriad Jewish pushcart vendors of the *chazzer mark* along nearby Hester Street (so named because you could supposedly buy anything there but a pig), to provide them with a safe, sanitary place to peddle their wares, protected from the cold and the rain, and criminal shakedowns. Over the years, it came to house a wonderfully diverse collection of food stands, shops, and miniature restaurants, representing many of New York's different cultures. But it is now scheduled to be razed sometime in 2019, its vendors relocated across Delancey Street into "Essex Street Crossing," another gigantically ugly "mixed use development," some two million square feet of high-priced "residential, commercial, and community space" going up on a long stretch of land. This space, in turn, had been kept vacant for decades as part of a corrupt political deal intended to keep nonwhites out of the neighborhood.

And so we come full circle, from the New York City that tried to help along its poor and embattled strivers, to one that would rather keep the land barren until the very rich are available.

The city is suffering from a 21st-century urban malady, one that Tim Wu, a professor at Columbia's law and journalism schools, first labeled "high-rent blight" in a 2015 *New Yorker* article. Prof. Wu found that whole blocks of businesses that had graced the West Village for years had closed: this in an area where the average per-capita income was over $110,000, and which was still filled with music clubs and expensive restaurants.

"It is both rich and vibrant, yet also now blighted with shuttered stores in various states of decay," he wrote.

Wu started his piece with an account of the closing of Cards & Curiosities, a twenty-year-old shop on Jane Street, in the West Village, that sold, well, greeting cards and curiosities. The proprietor, James Waits, attributed his shop's demise mainly to the doubling of his rent, but noted that the closing of St. Vincent's Hospital—sold off and transformed into another massive luxury housing complex—had also contributed, wiping out much of his business. But this is only another side of New York's—and all American cities'—ongoing retreat to the dysfunctional past in the name of the future. In the 1970s, fights raged in the city over the closing of public hospitals in Harlem, and other poor communities.

Now? We don't need hospitals—not if it means giving up a chance to develop even a block or two of prime land into luxury housing. Many of our richest citizens, in our richest city, can make do by visiting the sorts of street clinics once set up to serve the poor.

The empty city

The great threat to the New York of the 1960s and '70s was considered to be the flood of largely unskilled, uneducated African Americans from the South, and Hispanics from the Islands.

"Stop the Puerto Ricans and the rural blacks from living in the city . . . , reverse the role of the city. . . . It can no longer be the place of opportunity. . . . Our urban system is based on the theory of taking the peasant and turning him into an industrial worker," the racist *apparatchik* and commentator, Roger Starr, implored back in the day. "Now there are no industrial jobs. Why not keep him a peasant?"

(When he said this, and before he was rewarded for his outspoken racism with endless magazine assignments and book contracts, Roger Starr was New York's housing commissioner.)

This sentiment was articulated, over and over again, by many of the "gentrifiers." But the "peasants" poured in just as the hopeful and the desperate had always come, though they encountered, for the first time in New York's history, a city that no longer had many entry-level industrial jobs to offer them. The result was perverse, a New York that was home to over a million welfare recipients and featured almost full employment for everyone else; a town where the Bronx was burning down, but where seven million to fourteen million square feet of office space—then the size of the entire downtown of a city such as Kansas City or Pittsburgh—was built in New York every year from 1967 to 1970.

In the success story that New York is today considered to be, the situation is just as perverse: the rents are driving people and commerce away, but some of the tallest residential towers ever built sit all but empty. The cause is once again a flood of outsiders, but this time they are not poor at all but among the richest—and the most corrupt—people in the world. They have already proven themselves more destructive to the health of the city than the least-skilled poor, and their depredations will do incalculably more damage to New York over the decades and even the centuries ahead.

In the brutally Darwinian history of the poor, they either "made it"—got jobs, started families, became useful and productive citizens—or failed and were pushed back out of New York—back to home or to another place—or ended up incarcerated or even dead. The rich, though, are with us always, and now for the first time as a purely destructive, rapacious force, consuming some of the city's most valuable assets and contributing almost nothing in return.

In a moment of typical frankness, back in 2013, Michael Bloomberg, the city's billionaire mayor, said, "If we could get every billionaire around the world to move here, it would be a godsend."

Well, we all feel most comfortable with our own, don't we? But these are not your grandfather's billionaires. New York has always attracted the wealthy and rapacious, dating back to at least our most famous pirate, Pearl Street's Captain Kidd. Coming here was seen as arriving, for individuals and businesses alike. Long a "headquarters town"—as early as 1901, sixty-nine of the nation's 200 largest corporations made their home base in New York—the richest, smartest, most ruthless, and most innovative men in America vied with each other to put up great homes for themselves and astonishing buildings to house their businesses. They lined Fifth Avenue with their fairy-tale mansions—many of them later converted into museums, consulates, or renowned luxury stores—or at least filled luxury apartment houses such as the Dakota. They hired the greatest architects alive to erect gigantic advertisements for their transformative, world-conquering enterprises, including many of the most memorable structures ever built in New York, or any city: the Chrysler Building and the Woolworth; Lever House and the Seagram Building; Grand Central Terminal and the late, lamented Pennsylvania Station. They were *here*, and they wanted you to know it.

Noxious as the old robber barons could be, they at least dropped vast amounts of money into the local economy, in the form of property taxes and purchases in elite New York shops. They employed people in droves, small armies of domestics, vendors, and workers at all levels, to service their needs and their businesses. And they contrib-uted to the city through their building and philanthropy—Rockefeller Center, Carnegie Hall, the Morgan Library, the Frick Museum, to name just a few examples.

The new rich infesting the city, by contrast, are barely here. They keep a low profile, often for good reason, and rarely stick around. They make nothing and run nothing, for the most part, but live off fortunes either made by or purloined from other people—sometimes from entire nations. The Census Bureau noted in 2015 that there is now a huge swath of midtown Manhattan—Fifth Avenue to Park, 49th Street to 70th—where almost one apartment in three sits empty for at least ten months a year.

It doesn't take much to discern the same emptying out all over Manhattan, at least. Some fortunate friends of mine, thanks to a family connection, have an apartment on the 35th floor of their building, and of a Friday night in the summer we used to look out over the splendid ziggurats that line Central Park West and laugh about how many windows remained unlit (nearly all of them) once the sun went down. *Off to the Hamptons, the rich bastards!* Then we started noticing that the lights stayed off in the fall, and the winter, and not just on Fridays or Saturdays, but any night of the week.

New York today is not at home. Instead, it has joined London and Hong Kong as one of the most desirable cities in the world for "land banking," where wealthy individuals

from all over the planet scoop up prime real estate to hold
... as an investment opportunity, a *pied à terre*, a bolt hole.
Often, motivations can only be guessed at, because it's not
even clear who is emptying out Manhattan.

"The identities of the actual owners are often missing
from the paper trail associated with the apartment itself,"
Patrick Radden Keefe noted in "The Kleptocrat in Apartment B," a 2016 article for *The New Yorker*. "Increasingly,
transactions for high-end properties are done in cash, using
shell companies and limited-liability corporations—a web
of legal obfuscation that can make the individual who paid
for a property virtually impossible to identify."

As the headline on Keefe's article implies, such furtive
money transfers make New York real estate a perfect venue
for massive money-laundering schemes. A major five-part,
2015 expose in the *New York Times*, "Towers of Secrecy,"
found a mesh of circumstantial evidence to indicate that
dirty money was pouring into the purchase of multi-
million-dollar condos in the fifty-five stories of the massive
fourteen-year-old Time Warner Center in Columbus Circle.

"The building doesn't know where the money is coming from. We're not interested," a former manager at the
Time Warner Center told the *Times*.

"Sometimes they come in with wires. Sometimes they
come in with suitcases [full of cash]," a broker for foreign
buyers told *New York* magazine's Andrew Rice in his own
2014 expose, tellingly headlined "Stash Pad."

And New York, at least, makes it wonderfully easy for them to stow their ill-gotten gains. Today, as the *Times* has reported, the annual property taxes on an apartment that sold for over a hundred million dollars can come to just $20,000 a year, or less than .02 percent of the purchase price. And yes, you read that correctly, people do pay as much as a hundred million or more for a residence.

For most of a decade now, like lava flowing inexorably from some deadly volcano, the residences of the super-rich have moved east from the Time Warner Center to create "Billionaires' Row," the array of buildings on 57th Street and several adjoining streets and avenues that has dominated much of the Manhattan skyline since before they were even complete. These "supertall" skyscrapers—defined as buildings over 300 meters (or 984 feet) tall—include "One57," at 157 West 57th St. (1,005 feet high); 432 Park Avenue (1,397 feet); 220 Central Park South (952 feet); and, well on their way, 53 West 53rd St. (1,050 feet); 111 West 57th St. (1,438 feet); and 225 West 57th St. (1,550 feet). (At least a dozen others in the works are not *quite* as big—only "tall tall," not "supertall.")

Finished or not, many of their apartments were—at first—snapped up as soon as they went on the market. The *Times* used to tick off their record-setting sales in the "Big Ticket" column of its Sunday Real Estate section, often down to the absurdly exact last dollar and even cent:

The Old and the New: One World Trade Center and Cass Gilbert's Woolworth Building, "The Mozart of Skyscrapers."
Photograph © James Maher 2013.

$47,782,186.53 . . . $50,917,500 . . . $52,952,500 . . . $56,079,298.25 . . . $60,893,873 . . . $91,541,053 . . . $100,471,452.77! Nor did any of these records remain very long. In January 2019, the *New York Post* reported the $240 million sale of a four-story condo (a quadruplex?) at 220 Central Park South, a new building "dubbed the billionaires' bunker," according to the *Post.* It is—so far—the very largest home sale ever recorded, anywhere in the United States.

Who spends this sort of money for an apartment? The *Post* described the record-setting buyer at 220 Central Park South as "hedgefunder" Ken Griffin, "a globetrotting house collector who also owns a $58.75 million condo in Chicago; a $60 million penthouse at Faena House in Miami; $250 million worth of land to build a Palm Beach compound and a $122 million London mansion." Beyond the hedgefunders, other such buyers are reported to be Russian oligarchs, Chinese apparel and airline magnates, and increasingly, to use a *Times* term, "a mystery buyer," often shielded by a limited liability company.

In its "Stash Pad" article, *New York* included a chart of One57 and listed the twenty-five condos that had been bought before it was even completed, cheekily noting that over half of them had been purchased by LLCs, and asking, "Will Anyone Sleep in One57?"

When I first dared to raise objections to what this was doing to our city, I was lambasted for the crime of criticizing "capitalism." But of course what's going on in New York is more often an atavistic retreat to some kind of pre-capitalist state, in which the plunderers of markets that are far from free reserve even more wealth for themselves. It is something more in the tradition of the king's hunting preserves, from which local peasants were banned even if they were starving and the king was far away. Or to use a more urgent analogy, these areas are now the dead zones of New York, much like the growing, oxygen-depleted dead zones of our oceans and lakes, polluted with pesticide runoffs and smothered in runaway algae blooms.

Already, Billionaires' Row has throttled what used to be one of the more eclectic and delightful avenues in Manhattan. Along with Carnegie Hall, 57th Street boasted the graceful Art Deco Fuller Building; the New Steinway Hall, with its piano showroom; the Art Students League; the Russian Tea Room; the gorgeous little gem of a bookstore that was Rizzoli's, already a refugee from its old stand on Fifth Avenue; and the marvelous ramble of Coliseum Books. A steamship company travel office, where my wife and I once booked a trip to Europe. A diverse array of movie theatres including, once upon a time, the Bombay Cinema, New York's only Hindi-language theatre. Countless little restaurants, churches, coffee shops, and art supply stores, studios, and galleries.

High culture and little hideaways: together they made up a stretch of Manhattan at its most alluring, a boulevard that was at one and the same time touristy and toney, a place to browse and to slip inside, both European and unmistakably New York.

Now the Steinway showroom is banished to 43rd Street. The Coliseum was chased away, and died. Rizzoli's lived to sell books another day but its irreplaceable store, along with its entire building, were demolished. The Art

Students League, where many of America's finest visual artists learned and taught, and which proved a refuge for many
more fleeing Europe in the 1930s and '40s, was bound up
like a kidnapped heiress in protective scaffolding, while the
"Nordstrom Tower" at 225 West 57th St. was allowed to
build a cantilevered segment over it, hanging there like a
permanent sword of Damocles.

The super-expensive apartments along Billionaires'
Row will not only include many of the priciest domiciles
ever purchased in the United States, but also the highest
places anyone has ever lived in this country, more than
eighty and ninety stories in the air. Supertall, they are also
super-skinny, like 1,500-foot embodiments of the rich
themselves—"Clean favored, and imperially slim," as E.A.
Robinson wrote of Richard Cory. The Steinway Tower—
minus Steinway—at 111 West 57th Street, even has an
800-ton "tuned mass damper" at the top of its 1,428-foot
height to keep the tower from moving so much in the wind
that it will nauseate its residents. No need to tune any more
pianos, just the building.

Together, these buildings perch over Central Park like
a row of gigantic predatory birds. There are now so many of
the supertalls, gathered so close together, that they threaten
to leave the lower sections of Central Park, the only true
architectural marvel to be seen, in shadow for much of the
year. One simulation found that the shadows of the highest
towers may knife a mile into the park at the winter solstice.

When the journalist Warren St. John noticed that his
fellow parents had to zip up their children's coats as the
afternoon wore on and the shadows fell across the park, he
organized a community protest meeting. At this gathering,
Gary Barnett, president of the Extell Corporation, which
constructed both One57 and the new, even higher 225
West 57th, insisted that the shadows of the finished buildings would be "very brief—maybe they're ten minutes in
any one place—and cause no negative effective on any one
place." Fantastic! A park where people are merely strafed
by gigantic, looming shadows. Paul Goldberger joked in
Vanity Fair, "Given the slenderness of the new towers, it
might be more accurate to say that the southern end of the
park is someday going to look striped." But it's not nec-
essarily a joke. Landscape architect Michael Van Valkenburgh, creator of a "teardrop park" by the World Trade
Center, predicted that too many shadows will stress trees
and plants to the point where they will slowly die, over the
course of another five years or so.

"'Oh, why are the trees dying?'" Van Valkenburgh pre-
dicts New Yorkers will say. "'It must be related to global
warming or something.'"

As Warren St. John pointed out, the new supertall
buildings each contain maybe a hundred apartments—
most of them unoccupied most of the time—but forty million people use Central Park every year. A huge imposition
on the pleasure of tens of millions—one that leaves

children literally shivering on their playgrounds—for the benefit of a few hundred fantastically rich individuals, most of whom won't even be there. This seems to be the calculation upon which New York now operates.

The city turned in on itself

Ironically, the more the ultra-wealthy try to get away from us, the higher they climb into the sky or cosset themselves in their dead zones, the more they are revealed. It is the very nature of their skyscrapers, whippet-thin and tremulously high, that they must be made primarily of glass. They can be only so opaque, after all, and still allow a view of Central Park from one's marble bathtub, a constant cliché of sales brochures. Not opaque enough to keep us from realizing that nearly every one of these fantastically expensive dwelling spaces is riven by an immense, round, ugly concrete pillar, like something in a parking garage—the inexorable price of keeping them standing.

We can see how the rich live now, either directly, in video ads, or in sales showrooms that are partial reproductions of the "simplexes" and duplexes and triplexes they purchase. A late-night PBS half-hour show from a few years ago—in itself another corruption of public space, a thinly veiled ad occupying what is supposed to be scintillating free television for all of us—traced how the furnishings and materials for an apartment in a Billionaires' Row apartment were gathered and put together. Fabulous and rare though the accumulated materials were, the marbles and the hardwoods and the Italian granite, the meticulously selected closet handles and the table sets, the gleaming kitchen appliances and the bathroom sink, it all *looked* about as singular and luxurious and alluring as a suite in your basic Motel Six.

Oh, no doubt the feel of these fine materials to the touch every day, the views from the inside looking out, the comforts available at a murmur into the phone add something much more than we public TV viewers can ever fully understand. And then, these spaces are *not* made to be lived in every day, which may account for their resemblance to today's one-night cheap hotels, the furnishings for people who are always on the move.

Yet there are also plenty of resident billionaires in New York City—at least 53 of them as of 2014, according to *Forbes*, or more than in any other city in the country. Not to mention mere multimillionaires. *They're* not going anywhere, at least not for more than three or four months a year, and so the question arises of what amenities can possibly match the prices they're paying. What living space *is* worth $50 million or more, Central Park views on clear days notwithstanding, not to mention a yearly maintenance fee of $50,000, or $100,000, or more?

Perhaps because they are so visible to the outside

world, every luxury of the new super-buildings is designed to pull its residents inward, away from the rest of us—the very antithesis of urban life. Just as all the glass towers cut off wider views of the world, of the city, this is another way in which the rich and their developers have changed the essential nature of New York, making us more insular than ever before.

The elaborate ads for these buildings have created their own unintentionally hilarious literary genre. A single advertising supplement in the *New York Times Magazine* from November 2016 included 11 pages of this sort of real estate porn, a nearly endless promise of world-class gyms and swimming pools, spas and media rooms, libraries and cocktail lounges, conference and billiard rooms, wine rooms and cigar rooms, and *hammams* (a sort of Turkish steam bath without the steam).

Extell's "One Manhattan Square" on the Lower East Side offered a "Vertical Village," including "garden rooms and hedges, a tea pavilion, social courtyards and lounges, an outdoor kitchen and dining area, fire pits and an herb garden," plus a "golf simulator room, a squash court, bowling alleys, and the light-filled circular spa," and finally:

"An adult tree house and a sumac meander filled with birch trees will allow for lengthy strolls within the grounds."

One West End, at 59th Street and West End Avenue, comes with "a 12,000-square-foot rooftop terrace and interiors designed by hospitality visionary Jeffrey Beers, who

partnered with Scavolini"(!), and "a chefs' kitchen," while
the "grand-scale residences" at 70 Vestry Street, in TriBeCa,
enticed with "warm-hued Beaumanière limestone quarried
from the banks of the Seine River in France." (Not to be
confused with the Seine River in Dumont, New Jersey.)
The duplex penthouse at 50 United Nations Plaza "comes
with its own infinity-edge pool"—judging by the proliferation of pools and billiards rooms, the average luxury
condo owner in Manhattan is a combination of Esther
Williams and Minnesota Fats—while other "focal points"
include "the 10,000-pound handcrafted stainless steel stair-
case," in case you have a hankering to drive your Sherman
tank up and down the steps.

The extras go on and on, always grander and gaudier,
like something out of the ever more outrageous Gilded Age
hotels in *Martin Dressler*. The duplex penthouses at 30
Park Place boast "ballroom facilities," along with "gas-
burning St. Tropez French limestone fireplaces" and "Gaggenau kitchens." TriBeCa's 111 Murray Street promises a
"demonstration/catering kitchen." SoHo's 565 Broome
Street features "a glass-enclosed, 90-foot-tall landscaped
lounge and conservatory with a library and wet bar" and "a
'living wall' with vegetation" in the private driveway. ("The
building's curtain glass wall façade is composed of low-iron
glass," we are told, "with no mullions or joints on its curves,"
which is great, because I fucking hate mullions.)

"Private outdoor space" is the key here. In an age when

the amenities of the upper middle class have so improved, what better to offer the super-rich than this level of hidden, *in*conspicuous consumption? Want a drink or a meal, that swim or game of pool at the end of the day, a yoga class or a good book? There's no need to step out into the city. Something to do with the kids? Don't worry, there's no reason for them to go outside, either. All the best new buildings offer playrooms; the "grand-scale" 70 Vestry adds "an art area, climbing structure, ball pit, slide, magnetic wall and faux farmers' market." (No doubt so one day they can join the Future Faux Farmers of America.)

If this all seems a little backward—adults who meander through the sumac to their tree house, while their kids visit the fake farmer's market—well, it's your business, once you are hidden away behind "living walls." The emphasis on privacy is constantly stressed; after "hammam," the favorite word in these ads is *porte-cochère.* At 50 United Nations Plaza, the *porte-cochère* is "protected by a seven-foot-high hedge wall that encircles the entire building." "One Manhattan Square"—like most of the buildings for the very rich, this is an invented address that includes the number "One"—features a "private motor court" that "will open up to a Japanese garden, which extends down to the spa, allowing light to pour in." One can almost picture a modern master of the universe, stripping off his suit and dropping it behind him, as he strides through the Japanese garden and directly into the spa.

"PARKING JUST DOESN'T GET ANY MORE POSH THAN THIS."

Such is the level of privacy offered in New York's buildings for the super-rich that there is no need to expose even one's automobile to the prying eyes of the hoi polloi. My favorite fringe benefit, a luxury that has been steadily gaining favor not only in New York but also in such other favorite hangouts of the super-rich as Miami and Singapore, according to the *Wall Street Journal*, is "*en suite*" parking.

No, this isn't the infamous "million-dollar parking spot," complete with signed contract (and additional monthly maintenance fees), that Annie Karni first reported in the *New York Post*, back in 2012. That was at 66 East 11th Street which, in the endless self-parody New York real estate has become, was a former parking garage, converted into luxury condos—and luxury parking spaces. The *Post* suggested at the time that a million dollars for a parking spot might not be such a bargain, considering that one could get a $115 parking ticket on the street every day in New York—for 24 years—before equaling that magic million price tag. (The same condo also promised "heat reflexology flooring," "lighting patterns and air quality . . . designed to provide its residents with a better night's rest," and shower water "pumped full of vitamin C and aloe," so there was that.)

No, *en suite* parking is the sort of amenity that 200 Eleventh Avenue, over in Chelsea, offered up: a separate elevator for your car, which could be taken directly up to your floor.

"Parking just doesn't get any more posh than this," reported Sanette Tanaka for the *Journal* in 2012. In an attached video, she interviewed Leonard Steinberg of Prudential Douglas Elliman, who promised: "The garage and the elevator shaft sit behind two walls of one-foot-thick concrete, as well as two stairwells, and a hallway. So there are no senses of fumes, or sound, and it can burn for three-to-four hours before it imposes any risk on the building."

Three or four whole hours to escape, before your burning car turns your luxury building into a death trap! Apparently wonders will never cease.

The alien city

New York's great buildings used to be chockablock with beacons, crowns, ornamentation, friezes, and statues, pointing the way to the future. We did not always like what they were selling, but they made a public argument. The Chrysler Building, for example, with its brilliant Art Deco diadem and silver hood-ornament gargoyles. The Woolworth Building, "Cathedral of Commerce," with its terracotta tiling, glittering mosaic and stained glass, and cathedral carvings. Grand Central Terminal with its paeans to the history of transportation, its celestial map, and its statue of a glowering Vanderbilt. Even the wonderfully gaudy, gold-frosted American Radiator Building, intriguing enough to become a major painting by Georgia O'Keeffe.

By contrast, Rafael Viñoly's new, supertall 1,398-foothigh residential tower at 432 Park Avenue, which is taller than the Empire State Building and now dominates the Manhattan skyline from many viewpoints, was inspired by . . . a designer trash can, according to its architect. (Even worse, his designer trash can was designed by a confirmed Austrian Nazi whose most famous building was the *Wehrmacht* officers' club in Vienna.) For most of us, it comes from nothing and nowhere, just an extension of a pretentious, empty, overpriced receptacle, and it means every bit as much to the people and the city that it lords itself over.

"It certainly makes you wonder what other household objects gave Viñoly the idea for his next New York City condo tower," Margaret Rhodes jibed in *Wired*. "A metal ruler, perhaps?"

The meaninglessness of Viñoly's skyscraper has become standard for New York's starchitects. Hudson Yards features the $435-million "The Shed," formerly "The Culture Shed," no 21st-century Carnegie Hall but a six-story performance and exhibition space that is supposed to lend some cultural dimension to the vast development. The leading feature of its design is its "retractable outer shell," made up mostly of "tufted, Teflon-based sheeting" which makes it look much like your average air-supported tennis court dome. It can be moved on enormous steel "bogies" or wheels, something as vital to a major cultural structure as a snack bar in a cathedral. Planned events include "Fashion Week, TED Talks, and concerts"—a virtual compendium of the banal and pretentious.

"[R]uinously manspreading beside" the Shed, in Hudson Yards' "Public Square," will be "Vessel," the development's $200-million interactive artistic centerpiece. This is a fifteen-story collection of 154 connected staircases, which thousands of visitors can climb at the same time, continually passing each other. Not even its developer is able to take it seriously. Related Companies chairman Stephen Ross jokingly calls it "the social climber."

"Vessel," "The Shed," "Public Square"—in form, function, and name, the public spaces of the new city do not speak to New York's history, its heritage, or the desires of most of its people. These generic names remind one of that old joke from an earlier plague of gentrification, when it was put about that a new funeral parlor opening on Columbus Avenue would be known as "Death and Stuff." But then, the new city does not dare to name itself, unless there's a branding fee to be had.

The glossy magazine supplements advertising the newest buildings reflect this same strange meaninglessness that has become all label, no point. TriBeCa's 111 Murray Street, for instance, boasts "a David Rockwell-designed patisserie in the lobby called the Jewel Box," while Viñoly's trash can enlarged pushes a "restaurant by world-renowned design firm Bentel & Bentel." To the very wealthiest, it seems, the designer of an eatery matters more than what's to eat.

It must be admitted that, in the new city, the values of our public authorities seem just as misplaced. Those three whole new stops of the Second Avenue Subway that New York finally managed to produce this year, after nearly a century of effort, look remarkably sterile and devoid of anything connecting them to the New York that has awaited them for so long. In his fervent celebration of what is, in the life of the city, a miniscule accomplishment, Governor Cuomo heaped praise on the design of the broad, bland new stations as "a public space where community can gather and where culture and shared civic values are celebrated" and predicted, "This is just the beginning of a new period of rebirth."

What actually happened was that the new subway stations were outsourced to assorted stars of the modern art world (remember: in New York, everyone is a star), individuals who not one New Yorker in 10,000 would likely recognize by name or achievement. One of them,

Chuck Close, filled his station with mosaics, including portraits of "New York artists who have formed Mr. Close's wide circle"—Lou Reed, Kara Walker, Cecily Brown, Philip Glass, Alex Katz—and two self-portraits, of course. The purpose, Close informed the *Times*, is to "let people in on how many ways there are to build an image." Ah.

The artist Vik Muniz did Close one better, providing three dozen images of various friends, relatives, and cultural celebrities dressed up like "normal people," including "the restaurateur Daniel Boulud, holding a bag with a fish tail sticking out; the designer, actor and man-about-town Waris Ahluwalia," and Mr. Muniz himself, "in a Rockwellesque scene of him tripping, spilling papers from his briefcase," as well as his son, dressed "in a tiger suit, like a Times Square mascot on lunch break."

Isn't it marvelous??? The artists are depicting themselves and their celebrity friends imitating *us*, waiting for a train, and doing all the perfectly ordinary things that us ordinary people do!

It is one thing to replace some of the more offensive monuments and the messages from the past, quite another to simply blank everything out with the generic and the tragically hip. The artistic imagery scattered about the city—much of it now under review—features tributes to poets and novelists, generals and saints, fictional characters and heroic sled dogs, lawgivers, doctors, musicians, explorers, and reformers. It is also laced with a good deal of cultural, racial, and patriarchal supremacy, all of which could use a challenge. But this is no such thing. Our buildings and our public art of today are not a corrective but the easy disengagement of the developer, the inside joke of the already insular and elite.

The void in our art reflects the sensory deprivation of our neighborhoods, where the complex and varied city has also been wiped out. Where once the iconography of New York honored ideas, enterprises, achievers, and heroes, today's public spaces speak a secret language of the cool and knowing, an inside joke that is lost on the rest of us. The things that are lost will never be found again, and the new things we have received are literally empty, and spiritually devoid of meaning.

"What are you going to do about it?"

Boss Tweed, the corrupt master of Tammany, allegedly sneered this question when confronted about the 19th-century New York that he and his confederates so ruthlessly plundered. What are we going to do about a New York that is, right now, being plundered not only of its treasure, but also its heart, and soul, and purpose?

Bill de Blasio, our current mayor and possible presidential aspirant, was first elected in 2013, running against Republican Joe Lhota, a longtime state and city bureaucrat under the old regime and its ethos of development first, now, and always. Lhota ran a scorched-earth campaign, warning New Yorkers that a vote for some fuzzy liberal like de Blasio meant regression—meant going back to the bad old days of runaway crime, bankruptcy, and disorder. When all the votes were counted, Lhota had lost by nearly fifty percentage points.

Mural on the side of a building on Franklin Street in Tribeca, 2016.
Courtesy of Fredy Perojo / Alamy Stock Photo.

It seemed that the coin George N. Spitz started rolling back in that 2001 primary debate had finally dropped. After decades of conservative mayors, Republican and Democratic, hacking at the public sector—continually scaling back services and expectations while providing enormous subsidies to major corporations and real estate developers—New York had realized that it could no longer go on as it had. For the first time in at least half a century, the people were more afraid of losing their place in the city than they were of each other.

Vowing to be the mayor of "the other New York," de Blasio announced his intention to go right after the threat looming over so many voters: the cost of living here. The new mayor promised to "build or preserve" 200,000 affordable rental units over the next ten years, something that sounded like a good start. But the devil, as he so often does, lurked in the details.

Of those 200,000 units, it turned out, 120,000 were to be "preserved," mostly by negotiating with landlords to rehabilitate buildings that had fallen into extreme disrepair or were seized by the city for back taxes. Crucial as this sort of work is, it only stanched the bleeding. The remaining 80,000 new units of affordable housing would start with de Blasio rezoning fifteen New York neighborhoods for "high density" habitation. This is a solution that has been advocated by people from all over the political spectrum, even the liberal columnist Paul Krugman, as if New York were not already wildly overbuilt in so many places. The massive rezoning of the city that took place under the Bloomberg administration allowed new apartment towers and office buildings to spring up everywhere, even in places that will be in real, physical peril as climate change proceeds—a strategy that in no way whatsoever succeeded in containing rents.

Infinitely worse, though, was the other tool that de Blasio would use to coax the developers into building in these newly rezoned hotspots: the reinstatement of article 421-a of the property tax code. This has been the leading means by which New York has built new housing off and on since 1971, when the federal government largely dropped out of the business.

It works like this: developers get massive tax breaks on new buildings, so long as they rent 20–30 percent of the units in these new buildings below market rates, for the next twenty-five to thirty-five years. They are taxed only at what the property—often a vacant lot—*was* valued at to begin with, excluding *all* the value that their new building adds to the plot.

Sounds like a win-win solution, right? No one could ever accuse 421-a of discouraging new building. In recent years, 421-a has become well-known among New Yorkers mostly for causing landlords to add separate "poor doors" for its less wealthy tenants, as Extell announced it would do for its new tower at 40 Riverside Boulevard. (One is tempted to ask if the front entrance will be known as the "ghost door" for all those foreign investors who never show up.) But the greater problem, as Michael Greenberg traces, is that the tax break ensures that most of the new housing "consists of high-cost market-rate rentals, far more of them than would have been built without the enticement of 421-a."

This is, in other words, just more mass gentrification locked in for many years to come, while the city is further starved of needed tax dollars to maintain and improve its public services. And, at the end of that time, we can safely assume, the building owners, facing a huge tax increase, will do their best to drive out any and all remaining middle- and working-class tenants and bring in more rich people.

Much like the strategy of throwing money at virtually any business willing to come to the city and "create jobs," which culminated with the Amazon obeisance, the 421-a tax break is an anachronistic tool, one left over from those '70s years when both landlords and the middle class were abandoning the city in droves. Nothing could be further from the case today, and the evidence is abundant that continuing to use it is a *counterproductive* strategy, one that is subsidizing the wealthy while *diminishing* the amount of affordable housing available.

In practice, as Michael Greenberg reports, 421-a has actually resulted in a net *loss* of rent-stabilized apartments in some of the poorest parts of Brooklyn. The trouble is in part the definition of "affordable" apartments in new, city-subsidized buildings. Officially, it means that the rent is 30 percent or less of a household's monthly income. But, for all our great wealth, the median income is Brooklyn is still just $44,850; in the Bronx, it's only $34,000.

Most of the apartments 421-a created last year in New York, by contrast, were affordable only to households making $63,000 to $143,000, most of whom have other options in rental markets. The result, as Greenberg pointed out, is what happens when ambitious mayoral goals run into the logic of math. A recent lottery for a new Prospect Heights building, for instance, drew a total of 92,743 households vying for 297 "affordable" apartments. But, of that total, 65,000 of the entrants were competing for just ninety units affordable to families making $20,126 to $63,060. By contrast, there were only 2,203 applicants looking to win one of the 148 units for households making over $100,000.

"In a rush to rack up 'affordable' units and get to the 80,000 [new units] he promised, de Blasio appears to have stocked the program with housing for upper-middle-income tenants who don't need it," Greenberg explained. "It costs more to subsidize the poor because they can pay so little themselves; the logical fiscal alternative is to subsidize those who can pay more."

And even so, the costs of these programs are still incredibly steep. All told, New York City forewent $1.4 billion in property taxes under 421-a, in 2016 alone. Under de Blasio's plan, *at least $10 billion* in tax money will be forfeited by 2024.

This should probably not be surprising. The mayor's relationship with major developers—many of whom lined up to support both his initial election campaign and his 2017 cakewalk to re-election—has been so cozy in several instances that it was publicly investigated by federal prosecutors. No indictment was handed down, and in February of 2018 de Blasio did announce a new program under which New York will guarantee legal counsel for tenants faced with eviction who earn less than $50,000 a year. Previously, nine in every ten renters in this income bracket showed up in housing court without an attorney to face the landlords' formidable legal staffs.

This is a humane and progressive step forward, one that will preserve a roof over their heads for many working people. But de Blasio still seems generally oblivious (at best) to the wider, unintended consequences of continuing to subsidize new luxury housing. Despite the enormous costs of his housing program and its very mixed results, the mayor declared victory down the stretch of his 2017 re-election campaign, announcing that his administration would reach its goal of 200,000 affordable apartments built or preserved two years ahead of schedule, at the end of 2022.

De Blasio then added that he was expanding the whole project by another 100,000 units, with 60,000 to be preserved at below-market rates and 40,000 more to be constructed by 2026. The mayor attributed this "success" mostly to zoning changes and the 421-a incentive. The result will be untold billions more, in public money, gone to subsidize both fabulously wealthy developers and relatively well-off individuals who would like a rent reduction.

BACK TO THE FUTURE?

What are we going to do about New York's future? The right already has an answer, and it looks very much like a return to the past. Suddenly, in March of 2019, the Murdoch media machine discovered that New York City was on the verge of economic collapse.

"New York City is edging toward financial disaster, experts warn," blared a *New York Post* headline. The alarm was sounded by *Post* financial columnist John Aidan Byrne, who had been writing columns for months with other alarmist claims about "the exodus of New York City's endangered middle class" and how "NYC is the most financially distressed city in the nation." Several far-right blogs immediately took up the outcry, quoting the *Post* and its "experts" almost verbatim.

Those experts turned out to be a couple of obscure right-wing economists-for-quote, who railed against what they portrayed as runaway municipal expenditures under the de Blasio administration. Byrne, to his credit, was at least willing to mention the high cost of housing and government giveaways to developers in his own calamity howling. But his overall emphasis was clear: the city was hiring and taxing too much, and spending too much on employee pensions—a favorite target of the right, which has long advocated that American states and cities break their obligations to aged pensioners.

So much for the sanctity of the contract. But what is truly alarming here is how the Murdoch media syndicate was once again able to construct a narrative out of thin air and project it into public debate. Within weeks, this "story" was being duly debated on a local public television news show, *MetroFocus*, which featured yet another far-right Murdoch columnist, Ellis Henican, in an uncontested chat with host Jack Ford. Henican repeated, almost word-for-word, many of the same *Post* tropes about how de Blasio's wild spending and taxing and—above all—meeting of contractual pension obligations were on the verge of driving New York into bankruptcy, and already driving many of the rich out of the city.

In their remarkable dialogue, Henican actually claimed that New York had been infinitely better off under de Blasio predecessor Mike Bloomberg, not only because the billionaire Bloomberg was a financial wizard, but because "he had enough of his own money to cover any shortfalls." Yes, it's come to that: the right's latest creation of a halcyon past includes the suggestion that Mayor Bloomberg used to sit around like Old King Cole, merrily dashing off checks to cover budget deficits.

A quick check of actual facts from the U.S. Census confirms that New York's population is not diminishing but growing, and that millionaires are not streaming out of the city like Tom Joad and his fellow Okies, mattresses strapped to the roofs of their stretch limousines. A *Barron's* article quickly confirmed as well that New York's bond ratings were being upgraded, not plummeting, and that the city's financial picture was rosy, with investors snapping up its paper.

It should give us pause, though, that the Murdoch minions were able to so easily commandeer the public airwaves and evoke a response from a respected financial publication (also, incidentally, owned by Murdoch's News Corp.). The issues such a campaign is aimed at are plentiful of late: talk of higher taxes on the wealthiest New Yorkers, the resistance to Amazon and other corporate scroungers, demands for more spending on the city's working and middle classes, and anger over Trump's shrinking the longtime federal income tax deductions for state and city taxes.

We are being warned that, if New Yorkers don't pipe down and get with the program, if we don't stop all this progressive tax talk and get back to throwing money at the rich—well, it could be the 1970s again! Naomi Klein, in her brilliant history *The Shock Doctrine*, details how, for decades, and all around the globe, the right wing has taken advantage of natural disasters, economic crises, and its own military and legislative coups to institute far-right *laissez-faire* regimes. Not even Murdoch's pot-stirrers have the power to set off a catastrophe or run a military crackdown in New York. But it seems that we can expect them to try to perpetrate the next worst thing: rule by rumor and panic.

The transient city

Not so coincidentally, as Michael Greenberg also reports, landlords have redoubled their efforts—often illegal—to bribe or intimidate their less affluent tenants into moving out. Some of the more egregious examples he cites in Brooklyn include cutting off heat and hot water, inviting belligerent homeless men to defecate and hold drug parties in the halls; collapsing walls and ceilings; nailing up plywood over doors; locking tenants out and getting them arrested; and, in one instance, even bearing false witness to get a tenant committed, temporarily, to a psych ward. As a result, the neighborhoods themselves look much improved; it's just the people that have been lost.

In my part of the forest, thank goodness, the process is (a little) more civilized, a sort of soft, running eviction. The large rental company that now owns every building on my side of the block (and much of the next block as well) brought in crews of undocumented workers to re-point the brick, and thus drive up the rent for all of us by a couple of hundred dollars each month. Working out on precarious scaffolding in winter weather, these men were forbidden to talk to us, even when we tried to offer them water. As the older families do move out, more crews of the undocumented descend on their apartments, tearing them apart, right down to the brickwork, in storms of noise and dust that go on for months.

They cut through electrical cables and crash through ceilings and walls. Not intentionally, or maliciously. An overly zealous smash that shattered our bathroom ceiling even led to that room being redone for the first time in thirty years. What we got was the same deluxe treatment that the new tenants receive: cheap linoleum tile made to look somewhat like actual ceramic. Cheap wooden shelving and furnishings built to last a fortnight. All to lure the next tenants into accepting a rent that's two or even three times what my wife and I now pay.

I like my new neighbors. They're terrific people, just like the old ones, and drawn from nearly as many different places. Better educated, usually, with better jobs, but just as friendly and helpful. They tend to be younger, with younger families, and it's nice to hear and see so many kids in the building again. On the surface, in the *aggregate*, once again, this would seem to be what New York—and America—is all about: everyone moving up another rung on the socioeconomic ladder, the city filling up again with the next extraordinary group of people who will cherish and enhance it.

But I try not to get too attached, for I know that their time here is limited. It has to be, with them paying as much as $5,000, as they do, to squeeze growing families into 700 square feet of room. They are here only for a few years at most, until the next child or the next job comes along—until they can buy a place of their own, or the home company in France or California decides to stop subsidizing such outrageous rents. Then they will be moving on.

We are becoming a city of transients. Right now, there are two apartments in my building operating as Airbnbs; the only question is whether they are being run by the tenants or by the landlord. This has become an increasingly popular practice for many New York building owners seeking ways to drive their profits still higher by essentially turning parts of their properties into uninspected, unregulated, untaxed hotels. The potential safety or comfort of the rest of us—now living with night-to-night tenants who could be anybody—is not their concern.

The very idea of permanence has become anathema to our landlords, just as it is to most employers in this city, and this country. The same mentality prevails in commercial spaces. Rather than drop their rent demands even now, landlords are simply switching to short-term tenancies, better known as pop-ups. As Dennis Lynch detailed in *The Real Deal*, the real-estate industry magazine, this can mean "experiential activation" renters "looking to penetrate a conference or event crowd—occupy a space for four days out of a month." Or a "brand launch" that might last six weeks. Or a "target market launch" that averages three months. Anything from a day to a year, with the landlords reportedly enjoying the fact that such temporary clients don't require a long lease and are very easy to evict if anything goes wrong.

Between 2010 and 2014, the rents in sixteen Manhattan retail corridors tracked by CBRE Group, the world's largest commercial real estate services and investment firm, "skyrocketed by a whopping 89.1 percent while total retail sales for the borough grew by only 31.9 percent, creating what the commercial brokerage called 'an unsustainable situation for some tenants as rents surpassed what their sales growth could support.'"

Consider that for a moment: a growth in retail sales

of almost one-third, over the space of four years . . . succeeded only in making up about one-third of the increase in commercial rents that landlords were imposing. What's more, this price-gouging continued even as vacancies multiplied, a supposed impossibility under classical capitalist economics. The better business got, the more stores went under and were abandoned. The more storefronts that went vacant, the higher rents kept going.

In some of the swankier districts of Manhattan, this can mean the likes of Gwyneth Paltrow, Kanye West, or Tommy Hilfiger "popping up." In less glamorous neighborhoods, such as my own, it's more likely to mean the headquarters of a political campaign, or the ubiquitous Halloween costume stores that open now beginning in mid-September. But wherever and whatever they are, the meaning is the same: everything is temporary. The whole idea of a regular workplace is rapidly melting away, one more piece out of the idea of a permanent community.

We, we, we!

It is the impermanence that is becoming permanent. In September 2018, WeWork claimed to have surpassed JP Morgan Chase as the leading tenant of Manhattan office space, leasing 5.3 million feet of it at some fifty different locations. The international corporation, now relabeled

"The We Company," claimed a valuation of $20 billion at the time, and is making over one of the old, iconic Fifth Avenue stores, Lord & Taylor, into its headquarters.

What We does, mostly, is put together attractive, contemporary-looking work spaces for more pop-ups, tech start-ups, freelance collectives, temporary expansions of other major corporations (one of its clients is JP Morgan), and other transient enterprises of all kinds. Charging hard into "WeWorld," the company has also started WeLive, semi-communal temporary living spaces (often for those same temporary workers at the temporary offices of WeWork); a gym chain called "Rise" (often for—yeah, you got it); and even WeGrow, a for-profit elementary school charging a $36,000-a-year tuition.

Many of these facilities will be combined in its new, looming fifteen-story glass structure along the old Brooklyn dry docks called "Dock 72." (Much as the prophets of the new economy constantly announce they are bringing us the future, none of them seem to worry much about climate change and rising sea levels.) The idea is to mass-produce, on a temporary basis, what has become the standard, determinedly funky model workplace of the tech start-up, with gyms and kitchens and yoga instructors and (very often) wet bars readily at hand. The WeLive spaces are similar, with billiard tables of their own, and washing machines—and billiard tables right next to the washing machines. The eventual goal seems to be to meld it all together into a seamless, fun, live-work-play environment—albeit one that's completely transitory.

Oh, yes, and to change the world.

"How do you change the world?" asks Adam Neumann, cofounder of the company. "Bring people together. Where is the easiest big place to bring people together? In the work environment."

Neumann grew up on an Israeli kibbutz, and his partner in this enterprise was raised on an Oregon commune. Yet neither seems to realize that what they have produced is the exact polar opposite of a commune or a kibbutz, which are places where people with similar, deeply held beliefs band together and dedicate themselves to bringing those beliefs into a daily reality. What the We's and all their many predecessors and imitators have produced sounds much more like a regression to college—drinking, according to the *New York Times*, is vigorously encouraged—with a perpetual frat-house atmosphere based on a temporary association. When the WeWork "community manager" or your temporary employer pulls the plug, you're gone, off to the next gig, wherever that is.

I have worked in a similar space, in a former factory building in Manhattan's TriBeCa neighborhood. It was in a writers' room, on a floor—as was maybe the whole building, for all I knew—dedicated to various film and television projects. The facilities were certainly pleasant enough, and blessedly free of a working bar and any "change the world" grandiosity. But the room was intensely hierarchical—there was a definite pecking order as to how we writers around the table were supposed to suggest things, and an outer circle of assistants who were only supposed to speak when spoken to. Outside the room, the place was as bland and transitory as one might expect: the same smiling receptionist most mornings, a few faces who repeated in other rooms for a few days before their projects were over, and then we were out of there, work completed.

This is no country for old men—or for anyone, really, not wishing to relive the most juvenile part of their college days over and over again. What Neumann doesn't seem to realize is that what he is describing already exists: "a big place to bring people together" in random but fruitful interactions where they work—and, hey, maybe also where they live, and take their kids to school, and shop and eat and drink?

That's called a city, and it's worked pretty well for about 5,000 years. What Neumann and the many other proprietors of pop-up spaces have created is *not* a city, but a scrim on which powerful, wealthy corporations and individuals can slide across those people and those parts of a city they wish to exploit, without having to worry overmuch about anyone else's welfare. It's not a community.

We have met the landlords, and they is us.

So—what *are* we going to do about it?

There are plenty of immediate, practical reforms that *could* be instituted almost immediately, assuming we possess the political will to bring them about. The record-breaking $240-million "quadruplex" purchase by hedgefunder Ken Griffin in the late winter of 2019 provided momentum, briefly, for a "pied-à-terre" tax, especially after Griffin stated that he would not be living permanently in his new four-story condo but just staying in it when he hit town.

The proposal would have levied an annual tax of 0.5 percent on second homes purchased for over $5 million (that is, a tax theoretically starting at $25,000), and going up to 4 percent on second homes purchased for $25 million (or a cool mill). Under this plan, Mr. Griffin might have faced a tax liability of almost $9.6 million a year on what was reportedly at least his fifth real estate purchase in excess of $58 million.

The proposal for the new tax was immensely popular at first. But very soon, New York state legislators, liberal or not, were wavering under claims by the real estate brokers that the industry was weakening in New York. At last report, it looked likely to be replaced—maybe—by a one-time sales tax on such luxury properties, a notion that would probably cut potential tax revenues in half, from $600 million to $300 million.

Clearly, something has to be done about New York's property taxes—but what, exactly, promises to be the subject of unending debate.

In 2019, according to the U.S. Census Bureau, New York State had the ninth highest home property taxes in the country, with the median home valued at $293,000 and assessed to pay $4,915 in taxes. But these figures are distorted by the high property taxes many suburban communities have to pay all over the state and has relatively little to do with New York City, where the situation is much more confused, and arbitrary.

"Rental properties have an effective tax rate that is five times greater than single-family homes—and guess who the landlords get to foot the bill?" wrote Christopher Robbins in *The Gothamist*. "Glass-bound condos and co-ops built for Russian plutocrats and tech bros are appraised as if they are rentals in tenement buildings."

A de Blasio commission was put together in 2018 to study the whole problem, but don't expect any quick resolution. Few New Yorkers would begrudge the relatively low property taxes for any single-family home owners in the outer boroughs, but these figures once again speak to the need for some sort of tax to address land-banking and the proliferation of luxury condos.

Meanwhile, Michael Greenberg and others have suggested that we at least cease and desist with 421-a and other subsidies for wealthy developers, thereby saving the city tens of billions in tax dollars over the next couple of decades, and eliminating a major incentive for those New York developers—that is to say, all of them—who wish to build primarily for the rich. With that money, or at least some percentage of it, New York City could then build its own affordable housing—affordable for actual working-class people—without worrying about support from the federal government, or about 80 percent of the apartments going to more of the rich, absent or otherwise. An additional dedicated half-cent in sales tax—akin to how Los Angeles taxed itself recently to expand its mass transit system—is another idea for a permanent funding source. It would also be a good idea to keep rental apartments permanently rent-stabilized, thereby removing landlords' incentive to drive so many tenants out once and for all.

When it comes to saving small retailers, some have even dared to suggest reinstituting commercial rent control, the very mention of which generally causes landlords to string garlic around their necks. David Dinkins made that idea part of his winning campaign platform, back in 1989, although—as happens with so many winning Democratic Party campaign promises in New York and the country at large—once he was elected, Mayor Dinkins quickly made it clear that he had no intention of seriously pursuing any such popular measure.

Unbeknownst to most New Yorkers today—so thoroughly has even the rumor of it been stomped out—the city *did have* commercial rent control for eighteen years, from 1945 to1963. This was the most widely prosperous time in the city's history, an era that many still remember as the city's golden age. How much was due to commercial rent control is probably unquantifiable, but obviously it didn't hurt. Why *would* a law that benefited every person and enterprise in a city besides its wealthiest landlords hurt business?

Another good idea would be to restrain ourselves. For sixty-five years, from 1942 to 2007, New York apartment co-ops were forbidden from gleaning more than 20 percent of their building revenues from storefront rents, under the IRS's so-called 80/20 rule. Co-ops were originally encouraged as a way for working- and middle-class tenants to save buildings for themselves that had been neglected or abandoned by landlords. In time, though, they became one more preserve of the wealthy, and in December 2007 lobbyists for co-op owners managed to get Congress to repeal the 80/20 rule and let the co-ops charge stores whatever they wanted in rents. Since then, New York homeowners have been able to join the ranks of the most exploitative landlords, chasing out small businesses with extortionate rent increases no matter how long they have been there, while reducing or eliminating their own monthly maintenance fees and other assessments. In other words, we have met the landlords and they are us. This is how you create a city of millionaires living over abandoned storefronts.

For many years, attempts to actually institute any of these reforms, or to push through any number of other ingenious legislative fixes, has run up against New York's dysfunctional political system. Due to archaic rules designed mostly to suppress old Boss Tweed's Tammany Hall, a political machine that vanished more than half a century ago, the city's ability to alter its own rental and tax laws is largely subject to approval from Albany, with predictable results. Greenberg reported that state legislators from outside the city—most of them Republicans—are

East Village, Manhattan, 2012:
Material Possessions Won't Make You Happy or Maybe They Will.
Photograph © James Maher 2012.

routinely bribed by developers to thwart pro-tenant bills of any sort; from 2000 to 2016, city developers poured $83 million into upstate legislative races, "more than any other economic group."

Nor is the problem simply corruption, or the usual troglodytes from the boonies. The very idea of any kind of commercial rent control seemed to shock Alicia Glen, a de Blasio deputy mayor, when it was raised at an urbanist conference run by the Municipal Art Society in 2015. Dana Rubinstein reported in *Politico* that, when a poll of the audience found that 100 percent backed some form of commercial rent control, Ms. Glen—a former Goldman Sachs employee so hated by grassroots community activists that for years they threw a boisterous mock birthday party on the sidewalk outside her building—exclaimed: "Oh my God! One hundred percent!" and asked if there really wasn't "anybody in the audience who actually [has] done any real estate finance?"

Glen went on to assure her backward listeners that she was committed to saving "cool, funky New York," but that the rents currently ravaging the city's storefronts are "a very complicated issue, like most issues."

Finally, attempts to build *actual* public housing—instead of paying developers to build housing for the rich *disguised* as something widely affordable—will undoubtedly run up against the terrible reputation that public housing has long endured, and that has been reinforced by the heavily reported recent failures of the New York City Housing Authority (NYCHA). New York has long boasted both the most and the best public housing of any city in the country, something that probably holds true to this day. But since 2001 the federal government has slashed funding for the city's 176,000 public housing apartments and their 400,000 residents by $2.7 billion, and, for many years, the city's own leaders have simply let NYCHA's problems slide until now it has an estimated $32 billion deficit in making urgent repairs and removing lead paint—a deficit that the de Blasio administration is only now belatedly trying to make up.

There are indications that these circumstances may finally be changing. The liberal surge in reaction to Donald Trump's election led to electoral victories that turned the New York State Senate over to Democrats, and produced outspoken representatives such as Alexandria Ocasio-Cortez. The fight over Amazon, no matter how it comes out, has galvanized the city's political grassroots. Gov. Cuomo has finally been forced to respond to demands that he fix the subway, and both protesters and a federal judge forced Mayor de Blasio to announce a plan to repair public housing. Alicia Glen, abandoning her plans to run for mayor, returned to private life—sparking another raucous celebration outside her building.

Actually strengthening rent stabilization laws, winning commercial rent control, building new housing for the

Long Island City, Queens, 2017: "The City within a City."
Photograph © Nathan Kensinger 2017.

people, and limiting the rapaciousness of the co-ops
will be much harder fights. So will overcoming the long-
established habit of paying extortion money to the flimflam
men from the corporate boardrooms.

The prevailing idea that we now live in the best of all
possible New Yorks remains a powerful one. It is a ration-
alization, perhaps, to compensate for the frustration we
experience living in a system that no one really likes, but
that we have felt so helpless to alter, and for the angst we
feel at seeing the city—and the country—we love slip away
from us. Or maybe it's just a way to justify spending all this
money.

The journalist Ada Calhoun laid on another coat of
the Pangloss with her 2015 history/memoir, *St. Marks Is
Dead*, an entertaining narrative of one of New York's most
fabled streets and neighborhoods. Born in the mid-1970s,
Ms. Calhoun was raised on St. Marks Place by her bohe-
mian parents, and admitted, in a *New York Times* op-ed,
that their rent was $225 a month back then, while today,
"the same apartment would most likely be $5,000."

She asked, "How can music, art or beauty survive
when the only entity that can afford a corner lot is Chase
Bank, and when young artists have to live five to an apartment on the Morgan stop of the L train? Just give up on
New York, people like Patti Smith advise young artists, and
move to Detroit." But Calhoun herself wants to know:

"Who understands the soul of any place? Who deserves to be here? Who is the interloper and who the interloped-upon? Who can say which drunk N.Y.U. student stumbling down St. Marks Place will wind up writing the next classic novel or making the next great album?"

Well, it will have to be a drunk NYU student who can afford $5,000 a month in rent. What Ms. Calhoun and the other Pollyannas refuse to understand is that a bar is one thing, and a dance hall is one thing, and even a Gap or a Starbucks is one thing, but a bank branch is another. It is a carpet and a machine from which one extracts money and departs. No one is writing a novel about it, or making an album. Those things that we do not value, that we do not actively protect, fade away and die.

I used to hang out on St. Marks Place, back in the years when Ms. Calhoun was a girl. I was seeing a dancer from Waycross, Georgia, and we would drink 75-cent shots at the Holiday Cocktail Lounge, and talk with old Ukrainian men about the great middleweights they had seen fight, and watch the punks from the dance clubs play pool. Afterward, we would go back to her place in Brooklyn, where she turned me on to the joys of homemade curry and Patti Smith's *Horses* album, among other delights. Walking back from her place to Manhattan one day, in the midst of a transit strike, I crossed the Manhattan Bridge with a couple of winos and watched the sun set over the Statue of Liberty, a moment I'll remember for the rest of my life.

I did not believe that I was living in a utopia, or through the only possible iteration of St. Marks Place or New York City. But I defy anyone to have that experience in a bank branch, no matter how drunk they are.

No, the fabulously colored 1959 Cinderella New York of *The Marvelous Mrs. Maisel* never quite existed. But there was more cultural ferment stirring in one block of the Greenwich Village that her fictional self traverses than there appears to be in the entire country today.

An important literary genre sprang up simply from observant people moving about the city—or even listening to those who did—and recording what they saw and heard, day in and day out. Alfred Kazin's *A Walker in the City*. Phillip Lopate's *Waterfront: A Walk Around Manhattan*. Joseph Mitchell, Robert Coates, Malcolm Cowley—and, of course, E.B. White's classic tract, *Here Is New York*, which was generated over a summer weekend at the Lafayette Hotel. Does anyone even do such things anymore? Lock themselves away in a hotel during a heat wave to write a prose poem/meditation on the very nature of a city?

E.L. Doctorow, in his collection *Lives of the Poets*, wrote of how his father, "a salesman for an appliance jobber with accounts all over the city," liked to explore New York: "He especially loved the parts of the city below Canal Street, where he would find ships' chandlers or firms that wholesaled in spices and teas. . . . He liked to bring home rare cheeses or exotic foreign vegetables that were sold only in certain neighborhoods. Once he brought home a barometer, another time an antique ship's telescope in a wooden case with a brass snap."

That city no longer exists.

Cities are all about loss. I get that. Intrinsically dynamic, cities have to change or they will end up like Venice, preserved in amber for the tourists. New York City, for all its might, is no more immune to economic sea changes than anyplace else—maybe less so.

It could be said that New York has been gentrifying ever since a lack of space started to push its dozens of shipbuilding yards off the East Side and over to Williamsburg and Greenpoint in the years just after the Civil War. Many other industries followed, rarely to the city's disadvantage, unless you pine for the open-air rendering plants and stockyards that also proliferated along the Manhattan waterfront. Just as, I suppose, the older residents of Pittsburgh or Detroit don't miss the choking haze at midday that meant "prosperity" back in the day.

New Yorkers, over time, made just about anything and everything, from chemicals to bread, metal parts to chocolates, furniture to crates for shipping fine art, as well as toys and clothes of every description. Possessing the busiest harbor in the world for most of a century, the city moved things as well, all around the world. These industries were constantly in flux, but by the end of World War II, as the only great world city that remained unbloodied and unbowed, New York still had over one million manufacturing jobs, more than any other city on the planet.

These numbers declined slowly at first, then more rapidly, with about half of the old manufacturing base gone by the 1970s. Deindustrialization continued rapidly in the 1980s, until today there are estimated to be fewer than 250,000 manufacturing jobs, in 10,000 companies. Some of the last and most integral parts of the city's working culture are now finally fading away altogether. The Meat-Packing District is a euphemism for drunken club-hopping and shopping. The Garment District, caught between Madison Square Garden and the Hudson Yards excrescence, is dissolving into still more trendy bars and restaurants; the rag trade, so instrumental in shaping the very nature of New York, has been pulled steadily overseas for years. The same thing has happened to the makers of clothing throughout America. The advent of container ships would have spelled the end of New York's hundreds of miles of working waterfront and the tens of thousands of jobs it provided, no matter how much the city might have tried to keep them. For a generation, the piers rotted down to the pilings, while the waterfront crumbled into a drug and sex bazaar. Was nothing to be done?

Things change, people go. Favorite stores and bars close. The owner of that deli you love gets tired of carving cold cuts all day and decides to retire to Florida. So what?

The trouble lies not in the inexorable fact that cities change, but in our failure to deal with that change. Or, as Robert Caro once told me, "It's our job to preserve them—what's best about them."

Since the 1960s the prevailing critique of American cities, which comes from the right, has been the suggestion that our existing social welfare state was unsustainable. The question haunting our urban success stories today is whether the prevailing conservative addiction to privately owned, government-subsidized mega-development is sustainable.

Already, there are indications that the whole structure is starting to give way. The real estate industry was not just trying to wriggle out from under the pied-à-terre tax. There have been reports for almost two years that the condo market is softening, particularly at its stratospheric upper end. Developers have been trying to incentivize brokers with higher commissions and to tempt buyers with more of those fabulous little perks you get in America if you're filthy rich. The Madison Square Park Tower, an 82-unit condo at 45 East 22nd Street, for instance, was reportedly offering "to throw in two studio apartments and two parking spots for any buyer willing to shell out $48 million for the building's 7,000-square-foot penthouse."

The weakness may even have spread to Billionaires' Row. It leaked out in court that 111 West 57th Street may have been looking at a $100 million shortfall. All those sumac meanders don't grow on trees. And Extell's One57 suffered Billionaires' Row's first two foreclosures in 2017, including a record-setting, $50.9 million foreclosure on a condo contracted by one of those "mystery buyers."

For all the rhetoric about the need to bring in Amazon to diversify the city's economy, it has already been balanced on oversized piles of Jenga blocks. *The Real Deal* demurred from trying to quantify just what the outstanding—and the soon to be outstanding—debt is on New York condos, but claimed that "it's undoubtedly in the billions." If it should all go down, New York's ability to cushion the blow will be badly compromised by the fact that, ironically, it has already forfeited so much in order to spur development. Or as James Parrott put it, referring to Hudson Yards, "It is the height of fiscal irresponsibility . . . to provide massive taxpayer subsidies to a Manhattan luxury mall."

More disturbing than any potential fiscal or physical collapse, though, is the moral collapse that New York has already suffered. We the people bought into the same old song-and-dance from "bankruptcy" days that we weren't entitled to nice things, such as a thriving public space. All we could do was invite the rich in and hope they make it nice.

"Too often, life in New York is merely a squalid succession of days, whereas in fact it can be a great, living, thrilling adventure," Fiorello La Guardia told New

Yorkers during his seminal 1933 mayoral campaign.

Today, too often, life in New York seems like a sci-fi version of itself, in which we barely notice as our fellow human beings are picked off by the monsters living among us. Beyond any particular policy, there are basic philosophical alternatives to consider as we think about how we want to live, and how we want to treat each other, in New York or anywhere else—alternatives to the confabulated future that whatever tech wiz or workspace organizer would like to impose upon us for the good of his billion-something company.

A quietly magnificent 2017 exhibition at Hunter College's Roosevelt House, "The New Deal in New York"—part of the nationwide "Living New Deal" history project—displayed a vision for another way of life, one that Mayor La Guardia was instrumental in building. The exhibit featured the first public housing in the United States, built by New York City from 1935 to 1937, with funds provided by the federal Works Progress Administration (WPA) and Public Works Administration (PWA).

These projects—First Houses, Ten Eyck (now Williamsburg) Houses, and Harlem River Houses—were built on a human scale, just four to six stories high. The spaces formerly occupied by one out of every three of the rotting tenements they replaced were left vacant, to let in air and light, and to provide room for children's playgrounds and places where their parents could sit and talk and commune. The buildings were small in scale, and they, too, were no utopia—though they remain much sought-after homes to this day, even with the state of disrepair in which our uncaring leaders have left public housing. By 1941, a total of nine such projects had been built in New York, with 11,570 units, and over 500 of these developments had gone up around the United States.

Unlike so much later public housing, too, these homes were not envisioned or designed as projects simply to store the poor, but as integral parts of a new community. Their residents could take advantage of any number of other government-funded community projects all around them, from beautiful new swimming pools to refurbished schools and colleges. They could find work rebuilding their own city's infrastructure—or writing guidebooks on New York. They could attend plays and concerts of all sorts. In a country of 130 million souls, an estimated total of 150 million Americans attended free WPA classical music concerts in the 1930s and '40s.

The public institutions around them, and their own buildings, were adorned by murals—painted not by art stars satirizing them but by artists who lived among them—depicting the histories of their place, and their own lives. This, again, was not utopia. Marion Greenwood, painting her murals for the Red Hook Houses, groused about how she had to endure the criticisms of her work from both bureaucrats and tenants—"the poor American lower class," as she jibed—both classes of people who she felt had a much lower appreciation of art than did the Mexican peasants she had formerly worked with. But this was America, too—and especially New York.

"I hope the day is dawning when private capital will devote itself to better and cheaper housing, but we know that the government will have to continue to build for the low-income groups," Eleanor Roosevelt asserted matter-of-factly at the opening of the appropriately named First Houses. "That is a departure for us, but other governments have done it. Low-cost housing must go on in the United States."

Getting back to these first principles, to a city and a society that is thoroughly committed to providing a decent life for all of its citizens, is the only way that we will keep New York from becoming another Venice, frozen in amber. It is the only way we can regain "the great, living, thrilling adventure" that La Guardia envisioned.

New York has been—and should be—a city of ambition, and of contentment. Of the getting there, and the got, with plenty of room carved out for those whose desires do not include that deluxe apartment in the sky but simply making a living and raising a family by doing something useful—or not doing anything especially useful at all but existing, living, appreciating the vast urban swirl around them.

Yes, the rich will be with us always. But this should

be a city of workers and eccentrics, as well as "visionaries" and billionaires. A place of schoolteachers and garbage men and janitors. A place for people who wear buttons reading, "Is It Fascism Yet?"—as one woman in my neighborhood has for decades, growing steadily grayer and more stooped even as she remains unbowed. A city of people who sell books on the street—and in their own shops. A city of street photographers, and immigrant vendors, and bus drivers with attitudes—and even driven businessmen and hedge fund operators. Those who run the city should help all of them to get along a little better, out of gratitude for everything they do to keep things running and to keep New York remarkable.

This is what we must encourage. We must let the people who would force on us this sterile idea of the city know that we are still here, and that we will be heard. We must somehow get through to our leaders, who seem hopelessly invested in importing a race of supermen for the supercity, living high above the clouds in their tree-killing, supertall skyscrapers. Jetting about the world so swiftly and silently they are barely visible, if at all, leaving below them a city of glass houses, where no one's ever home. A city of tourists. An empty city.

Squatter's Sign in Alphabet City, Lower East Side, 1987.
Courtesy of Stacy Walsh Rosenstock / Alamy Stock Photo.

Acknowledgments

My thanks go out to everyone who helped to make this book a reality.

To Rick MacArthur, who first had the idea for the *Harper's* article, "The Death of a Once Great City: The fall of New York and the urban crisis of affluence" (July 2018), that became *The Fall of a Great American City*, and who has long given me a bully pulpit in a great American magazine.

To Ellen Rosenbush, my longtime editor at *Harper's*, who has always been a wonderful person to work with, as well as a true friend and advocate.

To David Wilk, my publisher and editor at City Point Press, with whom I am very glad to be working again, and who first saw the potential of a book here. And to Kitty Burns Florey, who was my keen-eyed, diligent copy editor at City Point.

To Will Stephenson, my *Harper's* fact-checker, who always keeps me honest, and does yeoman's work in keeping the record straight. To Giulia Melucci, who was a great help as always on publicity.

To Michael Greenberg, Jeremiah Moss, Jessica Bruder, and all the other terrific journalists and authors credited in the "Sources" section, whose refusal to accept the corporate line about what this city and this country are becoming has so informed this book.

To Jane Jacobs, "the gadfly" George N. Spitz, Jen Rubin, Gale Brewer, Fiorello La Guardia, Matthew Brinckerhoff, and so many others who have thrown their hearts into defending the New York City *that should be*, over all the years.

And finally to all of my cherished friends and family here in New York, whose company has, above all, made this a place worth living in, and caring about.

Sources

FOREWORD

Although New York hosts what is estimated to be the largest per capita rate of homeless people in the United States, it is no coincidence that the other American cities in the top ten of homelessness are also generally seen as affluent "success stories." They are, in order and starting with the highest number of homeless: Los Angeles, Seattle, San Diego, Las Vegas, Washington, Chicago, San Francisco, Honolulu, and Portland, Oregon. Collectively the top ten average forty-six homeless per 100,000, or more than twice the national average of twenty-one homeless people for every 100,000.

"The Shakespeare Riots," also known as "the Astor Place Riot" or "the Actors Riot," came about due to a feud between Edwin Forrest, the leading American actor of his day, and William Charles Macready, who was transforming drama on the English stage. Forrest, a thunderous and rather bombastic character, had long resented that Macready had turned out his partisans to jeer and throw things at him during Forrest's tour of England more than ten years earlier.

Macready—a more subtle, modern actor, who was much hated by his fellow actors for making them rehearse and read the lines Shakespeare actually wrote—then accepted an engagement at the Astor Place Opera House in May 1849. Forrest turned out his own fans, many of them rowdy members of local street gangs, who tried to mob the theatre. The state militia fired into their ranks, killing at least 22 people immediately, while as many as 31 may have ultimately died from their wounds. The actors and their rivalry was only a pretext for the attack. Much of the mob shouted threats and insults against "the codfish aristocracy"—the Anglo leaders of the city—and the rich in general, reflecting the bitter ethnic and class resentments already evident in New York.

WHAT A CITY SHOULD BE

The Bronx's status as the poorest urban county in the country is all too familiar a story. The statistics on it can be found easily, though here they were derived from articles in the London newspaper the *Daily Mail*—http://www.dailymail.co.uk/news/article-2905611/A-North-South-divided-New-data-reveals-poorest-counties-America-household-incomes-35-000-lower-average.html—and the ate, lamented *Village Voice*—https://www.villagevoice.com/2010/09/30/the-poorest-congressional-district-in-america-right-here-in-new-york-city/.

statistics on overdoses in New York come from the city's own health department: https://www1.nyc.gov/assets/doh/downloads/pdf/basas/provisional-overdose-report-fourth-quarter.pdf.

atistics on poverty rates in New York today came from the

New York Daily News: http://www.syracuse.com/news/
index.ssf/2016/11/new_yorks_forgotten_poor_income_
needed_to_survive_is_nearly_3_times_poverty_rate.html;
and the United Way: http://www.syracuse.com/news/index
.ssf/2016/11/new_yorks_forgotten_poor_income_needed_
to_survive_is_nearly_3_times_poverty_rate.html. The statistics on poverty in New York then—during the plague years
of the 1970s—were derived from an official congressional
report   on   the   city's   fiscal   crisis: https://fraser.
stlouisfed.org/files/docs/historical/jec/1975jec_nyfinanc.pdf;
https://fraser.stlouisfed.org/files/docs/historical/jec/1975jec_
nyfinanc.pdf;
and from the New York mayor's office: http://www.nyc.gov/
html/ceo/downloads/pdf/chart_1.pdf.

THE LANDLORDS ARE KILLING THE TOWN.
The one-man "Rent Is Too Damn High" party refers of
course to the inimitable Jimmy McMillan: https://www.
rentistoodamnhigh.org/index.html.
The figures on New York rents in comparison to incomes came
from the invaluable real estate blogs *Curbed New York* and
StreetEasy:
https://ny.curbed.com/2017/3/9/14854512/nyc-rental-
market-report-february-2017; https://ny.curbed.com/2016
/12/15/13967302/new-yorkers-cost-burden-rental-
market-apartment-list; and https://ny.curbed.com/2017/2
/2/14483418/manhattan-home-sales-market-reports;
http://streeteasy.com/blog/nyc-rent-affordability-2017/.
Robert Frank explained his "toil index" in the *New York Times:*

https://www.nytimes.com/2011/04/03/business/03view. html.

His figures are derived from this site and from several other internet sources: https://bidenforum.org/the-toil-index-income-inequality-laid-out-in-one-eye-opening-chart-868b51d3c890, and https://www.vox.com/2015/1/16/7545509/inequality-waste; and from Edward Luce's *The Retreat of Western Liberalism* (Atlantic Monthly Press, New York: 2017).

Jessica Bruder's *Nomadland: Surviving America in the Twenty-First Century* (New York: W.W. Norton, 2017) was an invaluable source, and is cited elsewhere in this book. The quote here is from p. 7.

Michael Greenberg's article for the August 17, 2017, *New York Review of Books*, "Tenants Under Siege: Inside New York City's Housing Crisis," was indispensable—a thoughtful, well-researched investigative piece that also offered up policy ideas and was written with real humanity.

SO WHAT ABOUT RENT CONTROL?

The basic regulations of New York's rent stabilization program can be found at the New York City Rent Guidelines website: https://www1.nyc.gov/site/rentguidelinesboard/resources/frequently-asked-questions-faqs.page.

Curbed New York provides a good history of rent control and rent stabilization (and the difference between the terms) here: https://ny.curbed.com/2017/8/28/16214506/nyc-apartments-housing-rent-control.

There are 27,000 officially "rent-controlled" apartments remaining in New York, for reasons too complicated to get into here, but that status is usually lost when the leaseholder moves or dies. For this reason, their number has been dwindling rapidly, and they will soon be gone altogether.

Another good summary of rent control myth and fact is to be found at the City Limits site: https://citylimits.org/2019/01/16/the-five-myths-of-rent-regulation-in-new-york/.

Michael Greenberg's *New York Review of Books* article was, here as well, a wonderful source for statistics on the number of rent-stabilized apartments and the incentives landlords have to get rid of them.

THE MEAN-SPIRITED CITY

For some general background information on the delightful George Spitz, one should read his *New York Times* obituary:

https://www.nytimes.com/2015/03/28/nyregion/george-spitz-civic-gadfly-helped-transform-marathon-dies-at-92.html. Accounts of the debate, the 2001 mayoral primary race, and partial transcripts can be found at these sites: https://www.nytimes.com/2001/08/29/nyregion/green-and-hevesi-exchange-attacks-in-mayoral-debate.html;

https://www.nytimes.com/2001/08/29/nyregion/diverging-views-about-policing-race-policy-taxes-and-education.html;

http://www.gothamgazette.com/searchlight2001/debate.2.html; and

http://nymag.com/nymetro/news/politics/columns/city politic/5082/.

A political activist, one Dale Benjamin Drakeford, who felt that Bronx Borough President Fernando Ferrer won the debate, recorded the results of the WPIX poll on p. 236 of his journal and memoir, along with his analysis: "Later on the 10 p.m. Channel 11 News, Connie Chung (who was the moderator for the debate) reported that the telephone survey responded to by over 9,000 viewers gave an overwhelming 'upset' win to none of the four more widely known candidates, but to George N. Spitz. He got an unbelievable 96 percent of the 'Best Mayor Choice' vote. The other four (Ferrer, Green, Hevesi, and Vallone) split 1 percent each. Did April Fools' Day come early, or is this an indictment of a lackluster political gene pool in the eyes of voters?" https://books.google.com/books?id=2F_ZPMIeadEC&pg =PA236&lpg=PA236&dq=george+n.+spitz&sourc#v= onepage&q=george%20n.%20spitz&f=false.

The WPIX Channel 11 poll was far from scientific, but the overwhelming result certainly confirms that most viewers felt Spitz won it—and by a margin that indicates more than simply fatigue with the other, less-than-charismatic candidates.

The specific incidents that have plagued the New York City subway system were widely reported. The local NBC News affiliate reported the G and F train problems (https://www.nbcnewyork.com/news/local/G-F-train-Meltdown-Commuters-Stuck-Twitter-Signal-Problems-477024113.html), while excellent accounts of the harrowing Harlem derailment can be found here, from Reuters:

https://www.reuters.com/article/us-new-york-subway-idUSKBN19I2CG—and again from *Curbed New York*: https://ny.curbed.com/2017/6/28/15885650/new-york-subway-harlem-derailment-cause. The stalled F train in a Brooklyn station was widely reported, and with particular verve in *New York* magazine:

http://nymag.com/intelligencer/2017/06/new-york-subway-f-train-gets-stuck-underground-without-air.html and *The Gothamist*, which has done a lot of terrific work on our underground: http://gothamist.com/2017/06/06/harrowing_a_f_train_video_nightmare.php. Also, my niece was actually on the stuck subway train, and survived it with her usual pluck and equanimity.

No publication, though, has bested the *New York Times* when it comes to delving into the underlying problems of the Metropolitan Transit Authority (MTA) and New York's subway system. The *Times* ran a magisterial four-part series in November and December 2017, titled "System Failure: How Politics and Bad Decisions Starved New York's Subways." It started here, on November 17, 2017: https://www.nytimes.com/2017/11/18/nyregion/new-york-subway-system-failure-delays.html. The *Times* has also run some excellent follow-ups on the system's many problems: https://www.nytimes.com/interactive/2018/05/09/nyregion/subway-crisis-mta-decisions-signals-rules.html; and

https://www.nytimes.com/2017/05/01/nyregion/new-york-subway-signals.html.

There has also been an abundance of good reporting on Gov. Cuomo's sudden disturbing intervention in the L-train tunnel repairs, from *The Gothamist, Politico*—https://www.politico.com/states/new-york/albany/story/2019/03/31/mta-abandons-full-review-of-cuomo-l-train-project-denies-ever-planning-one-942042—and, especially, the *Times*: https://www.nytimes.com/2019/01/15/nyregion/l-train-mta-subway.html.

"HOW ARE YOU GOING TO REPRESENT BEAUTIFY IF YOU'RE DOING UGLY BEHIND THAT?"

Here is an interesting article on some of the problems inherent in park conservancies, by Alexandra Lange, in *The New Yorker*: https://www.newyorker.com/culture/culture-desk/how-to-fix-new-york-citys-parks.

There has been copious reporting on the Business Improvement Districts in New York City and elsewhere, including: http://www1.nyc.gov/site/sbs/neighborhoods/bids.page and http://www.nyc.gov/html/sbs/downloads/pdf/neighborhood_development/business_improvement_districts/11_step_bid_formation_guide.pdf. The *Times* covered the Grand Central court battles and Justice Sotomayor's decision extensively: https://www.nytimes.com/2000/10/25/nyregion/after-7-year-fight-homeless-get-816000-in-back-wages.html.

THE MIRROR CITY

An excellent source for the history of Astor Place is Nigel Cliff's *The Shakespeare Riots: Revenge, Drama and Death in*

Nineteenth-Century America (New York: Random House, 2007). Luc Sante's *Low Life* (New York: Farrar, Straus and Giroux, 1991) is of course an excellent source for all sorts of nineteenth-century New York history.

Nathan Kensinger's illustrated article on Columbia's tactics in building its Manhattanville campus—showing exactly what has been lost and how dreadful the Renzo Piano buildings are that replaced it—can be seen here on *Curbed New York*: https://ny.curbed.com/2018/3/8/1709 5838/manhattanville-columbia-university-expansion-photo-essay. James Gardner's thoughtful review, in the estimable *The Real Deal*, of Piano's great botched opportunity is, while trying to be kind, a deadly accurate assessment of this mess—and, not incidentally, a primer on just why New York's architects of the past have it all over our current vandals—um—"starchitects": https://therealdeal.com/issues_articles/outmatched-in-majesty/.

Meanwhile, the *Times* ran an illuminating James B. Stewart piece on Cooper Union's bid for—what, exactly? Oblivion? https://www.nytimes.com/2013/05/11/business/how-cooper-unions-endowment-failed-in-its-mission.html?module=inline.

In addition to reading about any of this, however, New Yorkers and our visitors would be well advised to go *see* it. To stroll through the West Village, stand in Astor Place, take the No. 1 subway past Manhattanville, take a quick walk around St. John's (and check out the pay wall inside), and linger at the corner of 43rd and 6th. Only in this way will they truly understand how our city is disappearing into itself, and exactly how so many of our major nonprofit (and untaxed) corporations have used gaudy architectural "talent" to disfigure the neighborhoods around them.

THIS SPORTING LIFE

To understand the full scam that the Atlantic Yards development was, a good place to turn is Norman Oder's tenacious watchdog blog, *Atlantic Yards/Pacific Park Report*. *Crain's New York Business*, while decidedly more sympathetic, delivered a good blow-by-blow of the project, starting with this 2008 piece—https://www.crainsnewyork.com/article/2008 0306/FREE/809048612/atlantic-yards-secures-55m-in-public-funding —and continuing for the next five years or more.

For maximum entertainment value, though—and for a truly outstanding exposé of just what a scam Atlantic Yards was—check out Michael Galinsky and Suki Hawley's documentary film, *Battle for Brooklyn*, a labor of love.

For the hot skinny on the money that New York's baseball teams, major and minor, have extracted from the taxpayers, a first-rate source is Neil deMause, the longtime investigative reporter and *Village Voice* editor. The second edition of his book with Joanna Cagan, *Field of Schemes: How the Great Stadium Swindle Turns Public Money into Private Profit* (Lincoln: University of Nebraska Press–Bison Books, 2008) is a great place to start, and he also provides a nearly line-by-line breakdown on what the Mets and Yankees are getting due to the public largesse.

The *New York Times* has done some fine reporting on the

attempt by the Mets' owners and others to develop Willetts Point, particularly here—https://www.nytimes.com/2018/02/05/nyregion/willets-point-redevelopment-de-blasio.html and https://www.nytimes.com/2017/06/06/nyregion/judges-block-plan-for-mall-and-housing-near-citifield.html. To get an idea of the full grandiosity of the project, check out the report on it by the New York Economic Development Corporation, the source of so much sorrow in the city over the decades: https://www.nycedc.com/project/willets-point-development.

For the best reporting, however, on the vanished community that was the Iron Triangle—and on so much else—read Jeremiah Moss's *Vanishing New York: How a Great City Lost Its Soul* (New York: HarperCollins, 2018), culled from his blog of the same name and full of the soul, wit, and (properly) righteous indignation that characterizes so much of his work.

THE AXIS OF POWER

Moss has also written well about the cross-city axis of development in *Vanishing New York*.

Curbed New York is a good source for the facts and figures on the land-rush development going on in Long Island City, such as in this online entry: https://ny.curbed.com/2017/6/26/15875702/long-island-city-construction-usa-leader.

And The *New York Times* has done some outstanding work on the monstrous Hudson Yards development, starting with when it was first proposed but especially when the first half of it was opened. The *Times* greeted it with a whole special section, particularly the insightfully skewering Michael Kimmelman review it deserved: https://www.nytimes.com /interactive/2019/03/14/arts/design/hudson-yards-nyc.html.

The Bridget Fisher–Flávia Leite analysis, "The Cost of New York City's Hudson Yards Redevelopment Project," for the Schwartz Center for Economic Policy Research at the New School for Social Research, can be found here: https://www.economicpolicyresearch.org/images/docs/rese arch/political_economy/Cost_of_Hudson_Yards_WP_11 .5.18.pdf. It provides a concise, well-documented outline of just what the real costs of the Yards is likely to be.

THE TECHNOLOGY OF THE FUTURE—SIDEBAR
The fight over Amazon has been extensively reported in the mainstream media—usually by reporters and editors who could almost be heard choking back their tears over the fact that Amazon would not be coming to Long Island City after all.
Some of the more objective and informative reporting on the deal and its demise could be found at *Vox*, starting here: https://www.vox.com/the-goods/2019/2/14/18225003 /amazon-hq2-new-york-pulling-out; and again at *Curbed New York*, beginning with these articles:
https://ny.curbed.com/2019/2/18/18229407/amazon-hq2-cancel-queens-long-island-city-reactions;
https://ny.curbed.com/2018/11/16/18098589/amazon-hq2-nyc-queens-long-island-city-explained;
https://ny.curbed.com/2019/2/28/18245306/amazon-hq2-nyc-andrew-cuomo-jeff-bezos;

https://ny.curbed.com/2019/2/15/18226611/amazon-hq2-
new-york-branding-transparency; and
https://ny.curbed.com/2019/2/14/18224997/amazon-hq2-
new-york-city-canceled.

For a sane account of the billboards smearing Representative Ocasio-Cortez in Times Square, one can check out
The Gothamist— http://gothamist.com/2019/02/22/aoc_
billboard_tweet_ouroboros.php—while here is the outrageous Sienna College push-poll naming AOC chief villai-
ness for making Amazon feel unwanted: https://scri.
siena.edu/2019/03/18/2-3-of-voters-say-amazon-cancelling-
queens-hq-bad-for-ny/.

The pathetic "Partnership for New York City" ad begging Amazon to return—a low point in New York civic
pride—appeared in the *Times* on March 1, 2019. For a more
balanced view, it would be worthwhile to check out the local
Association of Housing and Neighborhood Development
take on the Amazon deal. And to glean some idea of just
what a callous and brutal company Amazon is in operation,
check out Jessica Bruder's account in *Nomadland* of actually
toiling in Amazon warehouses alongside exploited senior
workers and the company's malfunctioning, robotic "technology of the future."

WHERE I LIVE

This chapter is, obviously, based largely on my personal experiences living in the same Manhattan neighborhood for n
40 years.

It was augmented by Jen Rubin's lovely me

RCI and her family, *We Are Staying: Eighty Years in the Life of a Family, a Store, and a Neighborhood* (New York: Carb House Press, 2018). To read more about Dan Talbot—theatre owner, film distributor, and West Sider, who deserves a special place in heaven—pick up the memoir by his wife and working partner, Toby Talbot: *The New Yorker Theater and Other Scenes from a Life at the Movies* (New York: Columbia University Press, 2009). Or check out the extraordinary array of eulogies that greeted his death, including these: https://www.nytimes.com/2017/12/31/obituaries/dan-talbot-dead.html; and https://www.indiewire.com/2018/01/dan-talbot-legacy-the-lincoln-plaza-cinemas-new-yorker-films-1 201912040/.

And to get a glimpse of the beautiful old, vanished Metro, see *Hannah and Her Sisters* again. Or just come and walk through my neighborhood before the marquee is gone too.

THE CITY INSIDE: LAST NIGHT AT SCARLETTA'S—SIDEBAR

This aside is based mostly on an account given by Bill Moyers to Rick MacArthur, my publisher at *Harpers* and co-publisher of this book, and from my own experiences drinking, dining, and mourning in New York over the years.

BACK TO THE URBAN CHIC

This chapter owes much to the people who preceded me in thinking long and deep about just what is going on in New York, and why.

Beyond the invaluable Jeremiah Moss and *Vanishing*

New York, book and blog, cited again here, the research Justin Levinson puts into *his* invaluable website, *Vacant New York,* was—well, indispensable. Prof. Tim Wu's concept of "high-rent blight," as brilliantly defined in the May 24, 2015, *New Yorker* ("Why Are There So Many Shuttered Storefronts in the West Village?") was one I wish I had thought of myself.

Over the years, Manhattan Borough President Gale Brewer has proven herself to be a true public servant and an unswerving advocate for working New Yorkers, and her office's report on vacant storefronts can be found here: https://www.manhattanbp.nyc.gov/downloads/pdf/2017-12-14__Testimony%20on%20Commercial%20Vacancy .pdf.

Meanwhile, Russ Buettner at the *New York Times* provided what was both a damning exposé of Sheldon Silver's shenanigans on the Lower East Side and a fascinating look at how New York's *quid pro quo* politics work, in his March 21, 2014, piece, "They Kept a Lower East Side Lot Vacant for Decades." Silver, as of this writing, has still eluded prison despite two corruption convictions, thanks largely to the U.S. Supreme Court's decision to all but nullify the concept of political bribery.

THE EMPTY CITY

Robert Fitch's polemic, *The Assassination of New York* (New York: Verso Books, 1996), brilliantly defrocks Roger Starr and many of the other esteemed advocates of an all-white-collar New York.

New York: An Illustrated History (New York: Knopf, 1999), by Ric Burns, James Sanders, and Lisa Ades, is more than just the companion volume to Ric Burns's unsurpassed multi-part documentary, but a superb history of the city in its own right. It is here that one can trace New York's history as a "headquarters" town from the nineteenth century—and a "buccaneer's" town from Captain Kidd on—as well as pick up many telling and relevant facts such as how much the city grew even as it declined in the 1960s.

And, as usual, this chapter rests on some outstanding local journalism: Patrick Radden Keefe's "The Kleptocrat in Apartment B," from the January 21, 2016, issue of The New Yorker; the magisterial five-part New York Times series in 2015–2016, "Towers of Secrecy" by Louise Story and Stephanie Saul, on how so much foreign wealth—much of it stolen—has been laundered through New York real estate; and, again, Andrew Rice's July 27, 2014, New York magazine article, "Stash Pad."

Far be it from me to conceal any criticism of my work from the inquiring reader. Steve Cuozzo's July 28, 2018, real estate column in the New York Post, a Murdoch paper, calls the main argument in this book "deranged," and urges that anyone who might doubt that this is the best of all possible New Yorks check out the city from one of its many trendy, new high-rise observation decks. Be forewarned, though: it is difficult to find one of these eyries that charges less than $25 a drink. Letter writers and other critics have leveled the charges that I despise capitalism, or am a "not in my back-yard" naysayer. Rest assured that neither charge is true. I would love to see almost *anything*—and particularly a capitalist enterprise—fill the many empty storefronts in my "backyard."

Warren St. John describes his battle for Central Park here: https://www.nytimes.com/2013/10/29/opinion/shadows-over-central-park.html?_r=0; Margot Adler did a terrific written piece and broadcast for National Public Radio on the issue, https://www.npr.org/2014/04/23/305643904/nyc-s-tall-skyscrapers-cast-super-shadows-on-central-park; and Jim Windolf wrote a thoughtful piece on the fight for *Politico*, https://www.politico.com/states/new-york/city-hall/story/2013/11/central-park-and-the-billionaires-shadow-076998.

And of course, Jane Jacobs's seminal 1961 work, *The Death and Life of Great American Cities,* informs every line of what I am writing here.

THE CITY TURNED IN ON ITSELF

The documentary on PBS mentioned here was "The Billionaire Building," part of the *Super Skyscrapers* series. It was first aired on February 26, 2014, and can be found here: https://www.pbs.org/video/super-skyscrapers-billionaire-building/.

The *Times Magazine* real estate advertising supplement in question is from November 13, 2016, beginning after p. 88. But almost every such real estate ad segment is thoroughly hilarious.

"PARKING JUST DOESN'T GET ANY MORE POSH THAN
THIS."

Annie Karni's piece on "The $1 million parking space"—and the
other amenities of 66 East 11th Street—appeared in the
New York Post on May 20, 2012: https://nypost.com/2012
/05/20/the-1-million-parking-space/.

The Sanette Tanaka article and video on *en suite* parking, for
the *Wall Street Journal*, is from October 5, 2012, and can be
found here: https://www.wsj.com/articles/SB1000087
2396390444450004578002590988571244. Ken Belson
also wrote about it for the *Times* on December 2, 2011:
https://www.wsj.com/articles/SB10000872396390444450
004578002590988571244.

THE ALIEN CITY

Zoe Rosenberg outed the Josef Hoffmann wastepaper basket
that inspired Rafael Viñoly's 432 Park Avenue in *Curbed New
York*, June 1, 2015: https://ny.curbed.com/2015/6/
1/9954820/a-225-trash-can-inspired-nycs-tallest-residen-
tial-tower. Margaret Rhodes' smack at it in *Wired* is from
June 2, 2015: https://www.wired.com/2015/06/nycs-1-3b-
supertall-skyscraper-inspired-trash-can/. For some reason,
though, most of New York's design critics seem to have
assumed Hoffmann was just another Vienna *wunderkind*.
But Hoffmann supported the 1938 *Anschluss* of Austria with
Nazi Germany and, as a favorite of the Nazis, was given the
commission to convert the now unnecessary German
embassy in Vienna into a German army officers club.

The basic *Times* description of the Second Avenue Sub-

way art is here: https://www.nytimes.com/2016/12/19/arts
/design/second-avenue-subway-art.html. The interpreta-
tions are my own.

"WHAT ARE YOU GOING TO DO ABOUT IT?"

Mayor de Blasio's "victory" lap for "creating" 200,000 "new" units
of housing and his pledge to create another 100,000 can be
had straight from the horse's mouth, in this communiqué
from the Mayor's Office: https://www1.nyc.gov/office-
of-the-mayor/news/682-17/mayor-de-blasio-complete-
affordable-housing-plan-2-years-ahead-schedule-accelerate-
pace-and#/0.

The basic parameters of the 421-a program to develop
"affordable" housing through tax breaks to developers
are provided here: https://www1.nyc.gov/site/hpd/
developers/tax-incentives-421a.page.

The new, improved version of 421-a approved in Albany and
designed, in the words of Mayor de Blasio, to be less of a
"giveaway" to developers, is described here, in the *Times*, by
Charles Bagli— https://www.nytimes.com/2017/04/10/
nyregion/affordable-housing-city-tax-break-developers.html
—and, as Bagli notes, it was expected to cost $82 million
more in tax breaks than the previous version.

Once again, Michael Greenberg's excellent piece in the
August 17, 2017, *New York Review of Books*, "Tenants Under
Siege: Inside New York City's Housing Crisis," provides a
crucial analysis of the limitations of 421-a and the de Blasio
housing program in general.

One of Joe Lhota's shameless—and risible—ads

predicting the Apocalypse should Mr. de Blasio be elected in 2013 can be found here, https://observer.com/2013/11/new-lhota-ad-features-evil-looking-de-blasio-biker-gangs/, and an exposé of exactly how racist, demagogic, and false they were was provided by Leslie Savan in *The Nation*: https://www.thenation.com/article/lhotas-mistake-filled-attack-ad-depicts-de-blasio-soft-crime/; and by Ben Miller: https://nyulocal.com/lhota-badgers-new-yorkers-with-ridiculous-racist-ad-324457705f16. Mayor de Blasio was, as always, fortunate in his opponents.

BACK TO THE FUTURE? SIDEBAR

Here is the kick-off of the Murdoch press campaign to provoke financial hysteria: https://nypost.com/2019/03/09/new-york-city-is-edging-toward-financial-disaster-experts-warn/. And to get a good idea of just how expert the right-wing media is at amplifying its ideas, check out how the gist of the same piece was repeated, in one online periodical of the international far-right after another, often right down to the headline: http://matzav.com/new-york-city-is-edging-toward-financial-disaster-experts-warn/; https://www.memeorandum.com/190310/p57#a190310p57; https://bwi.forums.rivals.com/threads/new-york-city-is-edging-toward-financial-disaster-experts-warn.234348/; https://www.plow.io/post/new-york-city-is-edging-toward-financial-disaster-experts-warn; https://www.ac2news.com/2019/03/new-york-city-is-edging-toward-financial-disaster-experts-warn/; http://m.controlcalor.com/olga/9/20/experts-warn-new-york-city-is-edging-toward-financial-disaster-for-the-first-time-in-40-years. There are many more.

The March 12, 2019, PBS *MetroFocus* program that also seriously discussed whether New York City is about to go bankrupt—and supposed that former mayor Mike Bloomberg wrote personal checks to make up budget shortfalls—can be found here: https://www.pbssocal.org/programs/metrofocus/metrofocus-march-12-2019-x0ikb3/.

The reality-based refutation from *Barron's* (and the bond market) is here: https://www.pbssocal.org/programs/metrofocus/metrofocus-march-12-2019-x0ikb3/.

THE TRANSIENT CITY

For some of the most egregious examples of landlords trying to get their tenants to move on, I once again turned to Michael Greenberg in the August 17, 2017, *New York Review of Books*—and, for less egregious examples, my own experience and that of my neighbors.

Dennis Lynch wrote very well on the new permanency of pop-ups for *The Real Deal* on August 1, 2017—https://therealdeal.com/issues_articles/are-pop-up-shops-becoming-a-permanent-fixture/; his piece included the telling numbers here from CBRE Group.

WE, WE, WE!

The *New York Times* has reported extensively on WeWork in all its rapidly multiplying manifestations, including David Gelles on the rise of "We" and its founders' supposed quest

to "change the world"—https://www.nytimes.com/2018
/02/17/business/the-wework-manifesto-first-office-space-
next-the-world.html. Gideon Lewis-Krauss actually plunged
into the fully lived "We" experience— https://
www.nytimes.com/interactive/2019/02/21/magazine/we
work-coworking-office-space.html— and Michael de la
Merced wrote about the company's recent $2 billion in
losses, which it claims to be "commensurate with the size of
its ambitions": https://www.nytimes.com/2019/03/25/
business/dealbook/wework-loss-billion.html.

Forbes has also reported on the size of WeWork's
expansion: https://www.forbes.com/sites/heathersenison
/2018/09/20/wework-tops-big-banks-in-manhattan-
office-space/#275a72474b99.

WE HAVE MET THE LANDLORDS, AND THEY IS US.
The conundrums of New York's existing tax laws and how to
reform them were provided here in October 2018 in a good,
in-depth report by The Gothamist's Christopher Robbins:
http://gothamist.com/2018/10/16/property_tax_
commission.php.

For all those doubting that New York City ever enjoyed
a commercial rent control law, here is the proof from the
New York Law Journal: https://www.law.com/newyork
lawjournal/2018/11/28/commercial-rent-control-back-
again/, along with an argument for its renewal by Jenny
Dubnau at the Metropolitan Council on Housing:
http://metcouncilonhousing.org/news_and_issues/
tenant_newspaper/2015/september/why_new_york_needs

_commercial_rent_control, and a warning in *The Real Deal* as to why it will be a heavy lift: https://therealdeal .com/2018/09/12/not-so-fast-new-york-bar-says-city-has-no-authority-to-introduce-commercial-rent-control/. (As with pretty much everything else that needs to be done in New York City, it will mean going through Albany, alas.)

Raanan Geberer provides a good summary of the old "80/20" rule for New York co-ops, and its repeal, in the July 2008 online edition of *The Cooperator*: https://cooperator. com/article/new-options-for-co-ops/full. The main force behind getting the change through the IRS was Rep. Charles Rangel, the longtime, former Manhattan congressman and *poseur* supreme. No New York politician in recent memory was so adept at posing as a tribune of the people while in fact doing so much on behalf of the city's moneyed interests. The difference this has made is detailed by Hiten Samtani's 2013 piece in *The Real Deal*: https://therealdeal.com /2013/04/15/co-op-owners-could-see-windfall-from-new-retail-deals/.

Michael Greenberg's *New York Review of Books* article, "Tenants Under Siege," once again provided good ideas on what to do about the lack of affordable housing—as well as the obstacles to implementing any such ideas in the state legislature.

Dana Rubinstein reported Alicia Glen's rude awakening on commercial rent control in *Politico* on October 22, 2015: https://www.politico.com/states/new-york/city-hall/ story/2015/10/de-blasio-official-dismisses-commercial-rent-control-idea-027026. For the record, I deplore protesting at the homes of any public officials. But anyone who claims to want to save "cool, funky New York"—and uses that phrase repeatedly—https://www.crainsnewyork.com/article/20150410/BLOGS04/150419986/alicia-glen-hints-at-plan-to-preserve-a-funky-new-york; https://www.politico.com/states/new-york/city-hall/story/2015/01/alicia-glen-on-the-new-business-of-new-york-018673—is pushing it.

The *New York Times* provided a generally strong overview of the history of the New York City Housing Authority (NYCHA), which was the first public housing project in America—and has generally remained the best, even through the most cash-strapped years of the 1970s: https://www.nytimes.com/interactive/2018/06/25/nyregion/new-york-city-public-housing-history.html. Its abandonment by mayors of both parties—and primarily by the much-lauded Mike Bloomberg, of all parties—in the first two decades of this century was disgraceful, particularly because the city was richer than ever then. Nothing better illustrates the disconnect between private wealth and the public welfare in New York at this moment in time. It must be said, though, that the majority of public housing in New York, while fraying, remains generally safe, and superior to that to be found elsewhere in America.

Ada Calhoun's *St. Mark's Is Dead: The Many Lives of America's Hippest Street* (New York: W.W. Norton, 2015) is in general a lively and interesting history of a very special part of New York. But yes, Ms. Calhoun, it is dead. We can only hope with Bruce Springsteen that maybe everything that's dead some day comes back.

As to the history of the New York waterfront, I wrote something on it myself for the *Times*, "City of Water," back on October 12, 2013—https://www.nytimes.com/2013/10/13/opinion/sunday/city-of-water.html. Let us hope we may all still enjoy it in some form or another, through this age of rising sea levels.

My favorite quote from Fiorello La Guardia was gleaned from the definitive biography of the man and his time, Thomas Kessner's *Fiorello H. La Guardia and the Making of Modern New York* (New York: McGraw-Hill, 1989). It is a joy to read.

"The New Deal in New York" was a typically enthralling exhibition from Roosevelt House, the little museum and policy institute on East 65th Street in Manhattan, which consistently puts up some of the most thought-provoking exhibits and public forums in the modern city. As long as it is around, we need not fear that no one will be taking on even our most dire problems, and evoking our greatest triumphs from the past.